7 ESSENTIAL WRITING TOOLS

7 ESSENTIAL WRITING TOOLS

That Will Absolutely Make Your Writing Better (And Enliven Your Soul)

The Keys to Mastering Both
The Structure and Soul of Writing

MARNI FREEDMAN, M.S., LMFT

Copyright © 2016 Marni Freedman.

All rights reserved. No part of this book may be used or reproduced by any means, graphic, electronic, or mechanical, including photocopying, recording, taping or by any information storage retrieval system without the written permission of the author except in the case of brief quotations embodied in critical articles and reviews.

Archway Publishing books may be ordered through booksellers or by contacting:

Archway Publishing
1663 Liberty Drive
Bloomington, IN 47403
www.archwaypublishing.com
1 (888) 242-5904

Because of the dynamic nature of the Internet, any web addresses or links contained in this book may have changed since publication and may no longer be valid. The views expressed in this work are solely those of the author and do not necessarily reflect the views of the publisher, and the publisher hereby disclaims any responsibility for them.

Any people depicted in stock imagery provided by Thinkstock are models, and such images are being used for illustrative purposes only. Certain stock imagery © Thinkstock.

ISBN: 978-1-4808-2308-2 (sc)
ISBN: 978-1-4808-2310-5 (hc)
ISBN: 978-1-4808-2309-9 (e)

Library of Congress Control Number: 2015918205

Print information available on the last page.

Archway Publishing rev. date: 2/10/2016

Contents

Should I Be Writing? xiii
All the Beginning Stuff xiv
What Writers Can Learn From Pirates xvii
Frequently Asked Questions xxii
The 11 Commandments for Writing a First Draft xxiii
Infrequently Asked Questions xxix

Tool #1: Your Tenacious WRITING ROUTINE

No One Wants to Buy Boy Scout Popcorn 3
Tenacity—It's a Life Shift 5
What Kind of Writer Are You? 8
Uncover Your Creative Process 10
How to Investigate Your Best Writing Habits and Make Them Stick 14
Incorporate Play Into Your Writing Routine 17
Incorporate Positive Thinking Into Your Routine 18
Phases of Transformation 21
Madonna and Miguel → Two Writers Reveal How They Used the Phases of Transformation 30
What If, What If, What If? 34
Ideas to Up Your Inspiration 36
Your Tenacious Writing Routine 42
Takeaway Lessons for Tool #1 43

Tool #2: Creating a Solid STORY IDEA

The Drunk Man Has a Point 47
Creating the Strongest Story Idea Possible 51
Two Real Writers, Mary and Paul, Share Their Process to
   Find Solid Story Ideas 58
Extra Credit! 66
Knowing Your Umbrella Theme 68
Umbrella Theme Inspiration 70
Solid Story Idea Worksheet 77
Takeaway Lessons for Tool #2 78

Tool #3: Dynamic CHARACTER Creation

Oh, I Got the Villain. Boy, Do I Have the Villain! 85
9 Character Elements Worksheet 87
Frequently Asked Questions About the 9 Character
   Elements Worksheet 88
Characters' Roles/Terms to Know 90
The Darker Side of Heroes, The Lighter Side of Villains 95
Put a Face on It 101
Yo Mama So… 104
Character Arc Table 114
Tips to Crafting a Real, Believable Arc 120
THE BIG 55 Character Archetypes From A–Z 129
Extra Credit! 138
9 Character Elements Worksheet 139
Takeaway Lessons for Tool #3 140

Tool #4: Defining the SHAPE of Your Story

"I'm Blind, I Tell You, I'm Blind!" 146
Do You Know These Five Guys? 151
Key Spot #1: The Ending 154
Key Spot #2: The Climax 161
Key Spot #3: The Catalyst 163
Story Shape Worksheet 167
Takeaway Lessons for Tool #4 168

Tool #5: PLOT AND POUR Structure for Everything From Novels to Memoirs

The Incident 174
15 Essential Plot Spots 185
15 Plot Spots Worksheet 211
Instructions for Pouring 212
Takeaway Lessons for Tool #5 216

Tool #6: Writing the Compelling SCENE with Depth, Originality and Special Sauce

Checklist for Effective Scene Writing 220
Sequels! 245
Just a Smidge About Dialogue 249
Marni's Secrets About Getting to the Juice of a Scene 251
Worksheet for Effective Scene Writing 256
Takeaway Lessons for Tool #6 257

Tool #7: Defining (and Using) Your VOICE
Uncovering the Soul of Your Work

"Don't Send Me Anything With Unicorns." 262
My Name Is Mittens and I'm Totally Confused 265
Listen, Play and Watch Out for Shame 269
DIG → MIX → LAUNCH 3 Steps to Finding (and Using)
 Your Voice 274
Play Exercise: The Free Word Grab 278
Practice Standing in the Light of Your Truth 283
Fail Big 286
Worksheet to Uncover Your Writer's Voice 296
Takeaway Lessons for Tool #7 297
In Conclusion 299

Appendixes

Appendix 1. Troubleshooting a Common "Writerly" Issue 305
Appendix 2. More 15 Plot Spots Examples: *Harry Potter and
 the Sorcerer's Stone*, *Pride and Prejudice* and
 Thelma and Louise 309
Appendix 3. More Tools I Couldn't Stuff Anywhere Else 323
Acknowledgments and Credits 333

These tools will teach you how to:
brainstorm,
outline
and tenaciously write
at your highest level possible.

Dedicated to…

Two tenacious moms: Natalie Freedman and Jeannie Jones. My mother, Natalie, continues to give me the courage to have a boundless spirit, a love for creativity and the tenacious chutzpah to jump into the deep end of the pool (over and over again). Jeannie was my best friend's mother, and I didn't know her that well. In fact, she didn't like me much as a young girl (she thought I was a bad influence), but she came around. She passed almost 10 years ago, and she's been my, and my editor Tracy's, angel ever since.

Special thanks to…

Ben (best little man in the whole world), Carlos (my soulmate), Tracy, Dad and my sisters, who each believed in me in their own way—and this went a long way. To my writing groups and students: Your energy keeps me alive and excited about the craft. You reveal to me, again and again, how blessed I am to watch something wonderful bloom as my profession.

Why This Book?

There are so many friggin' books on writing. I know. I've probably read most of them. So why should you read this one?

1. I understand the bitch that is writing.

2. I can be exceptionally lazy, and I've spent years making complex ideas simpler; I'm always on the lookout for a shortcut.

3. I'm providing you with worksheets that work. I've used them personally, and hundreds of my clients and students have used them.

4. I understand writing from all sides of the game, having been a screenwriter, book writer, blog writer, agent, professional reader, editor, script doctor, writing teacher and writing coach. I'm presenting you with tools that were cultivated based on the needs of the writer as well as the needs of the marketplace.

5. I'm also a therapist. I don't know why this is important, but it seems to help people I work with. Maybe something about how writers and therapists have to understand human behavior.

6. I'm not full of it. I really believe in this stuff.

7. I want you to fall in love with the magic that is writing, not just the nuts-and-bolts tools. This book is a combination of the hard stuff and the squishy stuff— hopefully, in just the right amounts.

How I Hope to Help Unlock Something Powerful Within You:

When I first started out at the USC School of Film eight thousand years ago, I was convinced that you couldn't have both structure and soul. I believed that writing either contained structure OR soul.

Years of experience on all sides of the game have taught me that the delicate marriage between the two is where the magic lies. The goal of this book is to help writers master the essential creative building blocks all writers should know (Structure) and to express their voice with vulnerability, authenticity and, my favorite, tenacity (Soul).

If you stick with me on this journey, there is no doubt about it, you will elevate your craft.

STRUCTURAL TOOLS + YOUR SOUL = MAGIC

Should I Be Writing?

Ask yourself

1. Do you feel like you have a story or an idea that simply must come out, must be expressed?
2. Does it just "feel right" to take pen to paper?
3. Do you feel happy or like you have accomplished something real after you have completed a piece of writing?
4. Do you feel compelled to share a message?
5. Do you feel bad (or does some pressure build up) when you don't write?
6. Do you feel like some part of you is "home" when you write or when you are around other writers?

If you answered "yes" to any of these questions, then, chances are, you are a writer.

And, if you are a writer, you are going to need some tools to get a leg up. This book will be helpful for the beginning writer as well as the advanced writer.

The information presented is a synthesis of what I believe are the seven most essential writing tools that encompass the heart and craft of writing. These are the ones I can't live without.

And neither should you.

Be prepared to grow in ways you cannot imagine.

The journey of a writer is as deep and rich as they come.

All the Beginning Stuff

Why Did I Write This Book?

After 20 years of teaching, speaking, editing and coaching writers, along with 12 years of working as a therapist for artists and writers, I have amassed a caldron of knowledge. (Yeah, I'm totally a good witch of writing.)

I have learned from some amazing teachers, students and master storytellers.

Being someone whose total passion is to teach other writers, I have learned that almost all writers fall into similar traps and pitfalls. For some reason, we writers fight the same unnecessary fights on our way to writing gold.

Over the years, I have learned a few things about writers:

- The quick and dirty truth is that writers resist the basics.
- Writers often shortchange the "personal brainstorming" period.
- Most writers do not know what type of writer they are or what their particular process might be, and, therefore, they often don't know *how they actually work*.
- Most writers do not know how to balance the need for structure with their spontaneous creative spirit.
- Most writers do not know how to access their voice, and they suppress their desire to risk.
- Most writers don't know how to blend structure and soul.
- Most writers give up too soon.

Where Does It All Go Wrong?

Resisting and/or forgetting the basics are where I see the majority of writers go down the rabbit hole. We get fancy. We want to follow our own lead. We get neurotic, hurried and impatient. More times than not, I can find the answer to a writer's problem by simply going back to the basics. In fact, brilliance often occurs when writers return to the building blocks.

But even knowing and utilizing the building blocks is not enough to compete in today's marketplace. To truly create a standout piece of writing, it must stem from the soul of the writer. It must be in the writer's voice. And this means that the writer must take risks.

Why Structure and Soul?

Structure and soul are the yin and the yang of writing. When they are interwoven, they work to create a fabric that can be both sturdy and uniquely surprising. Tool #5—The Plot and Pour Tool—can radically alter the way you approach your craft.

So, to sum it all up, I wrote this book in the hopes of helping writers to both embrace the building blocks of writing and to risk expressing their voices in the process.

How to Use This Book

First, an important note: If anything in this book makes you want to stop writing, then toss the book aside. The most important part of writing is writing—no matter how or when you do it. Stay in motion.

A bit about the structure of the book…

Each tool contains

- A corresponding worksheet to help you work through/learn the tool.
- Examples of how other writers have used the tools.
- Bottom-line takeaway lessons.

This is a build-your-own-experience kind of book.

You can read this book from beginning to end, or you can skip around to the parts you find most inspiring.

There is no one "right" way to begin the writing process. Inspiration comes from a variety of sources. Some writers begin with dialogue. Others draw inspiration from their nonsensical dreams or from their wacky Aunt Susan or from the bold work of writers they admire. A few writers I know outline their plots from beginning to end before putting words on the page. (If you can do this, you will save yourself a lot of time, but more on that later.)

While there is no one way *into* a story, there is a big, fat and extremely common mistake that most beginning writers make.

Writers write too soon, without thinking things through.

What Writers Can Learn From Pirates

I have a thing for pirates. It started about three years ago when my son (then 5) got a pirate play set. It came with a cool hat, some gold, a sword and, of course, an eye patch. But it also came with a big, beautiful treasure map.

That morning, I had been working with a talented memoir writer who was on her second book. She was stuck. She had been writing aimlessly for months in the hopes of trying to find out where her story was leading her. She had only a vague idea of what she wanted, wasn't sure how to get there and, truthfully, she was afraid of being honest about her story. She was afraid to take any big risks. This writer—lost but full of talent and promise—was like many of the writers who had knocked on my door.

My son went about playing. He hid all the super-shiny gold pieces under his bed. Then he grabbed an old cardboard box from his closet.

"What are you doing?" I asked.

"Duh, Mom, I'm making a ship. I'm going to find the treasure." My son then grabbed a plastic bat (for his paddle) and climbed inside the box. He began the long journey from one end of the room to the bed on the opposite side, where the treasure was hidden.

In the middle of the journey, he groaned. He turned the box around and started paddling back.

Once back, he grabbed the map, peered at it intensely and then he got back in.

As I watched him play, it was as if the angels began to sing. Epiphany.

Pirates know exactly what they want. Treasure. And, in general, (I am now sort of a pirate expert), most pirates don't like to wander around aimlessly in search of said treasure. Generally, pirates carry a map. A map marked with a big red "X." Smart thinking. They know what they want, and they have instructions to get it.

The last reason I like pirates is that they are not afraid to be who they are. They curse and spit and say what's on their mind. They let it all hang out.

A good writer (and a good pirate) is one who

- Knows where they are headed.
- Has some sort of map.
- Is willing to be authentic, to let it all hang out.

(If you are reading something into the fact that my son hid the gold from himself, you are right on track. We writers often hide our treasure from ourselves. But thankfully, this also means that we can find it.)

Where Things Go Wonky

Let's say you were an anxious pirate who was so excited to get going that you left shore without thinking much about where you were going or how you might get there (you got in the box without the map). At first, you may find yourself thinking, "*Who needs a map when you have the spirit of adventure filling your heart and soul?"* You may feel that it's a lot more fun just to jump in and see where the journey leads!

As you and your surly crew make your way out to sea, you may initially find your journey to be a joyful, freeing experience. You may even be seeing beautiful new sights, making new discoveries and enjoying the spontaneity of the moment.

But then, a few months go by.

The shininess of the journey will probably have worn off and, most likely, you'd like to find some gold. You may begin to realize that you might be a little lost. Your crew may start to get a little cranky. You will probably start to wish that you had that darn map.

A Sad but True Fact

Wandering pirates have a much lower success rate than pirates with maps.

So, what I'm trying to say is that even though you don't need to read the tools in any particular order, you should read all the tools before putting pen to paper. And more importantly: **Think through your idea frontways and back before you get serious.**

While skipping all the planning and rushing to put words on paper may feel fun or like "true writing," there is a cost to writing without planning. Often the piece falls apart in the middle, has flat characters or has an ultimately unsatisfying ending.

All writers must rewrite. But writers that don't take some initial thinking time end up rewriting a hell of a lot more. Sometimes they even scrap their first draft entirely.

Having said all that, I fully understand what it is to be "structure resistant." I was myself for many years, having fought the wisdom of my USC film-writing teachers with everything I had. Then I spent years fighting managers, producers and agents. It was a big waste of time. When I embraced structure, the world of storytelling opened up to me.

So is there another way, a more balanced approach? I say yes. I call it "Plot and Pour," and I will teach you how to do it in Tool #5. Once you learn this tool, you will know where you are going, and you will still get to have tons of fun getting there.

If you feel that you too are structure resistant, focus less on the full plotting tool and more on the section about shaping your story (so your story will have rising conflict that peaks into a climax and results in a satisfying ending). Do your best while you are in the "personal brainstorming" stage to date your ideas for a while—but no getting married just yet.

Your best piece of writing stems from a collection of your BEST ideas, not a collection of your FIRST ideas. The truth is that even thinking about the shape of your story will greatly reduce the amount of time you will have to spend rewriting. If you are new to plotting and structuring your story, I say hey, plotting is very much like Green Eggs and Ham (you may actually like it).

Is there ever a time to ditch the map and write whatever wants to come out?

Yes. And often.

That is the *pouring* part of Plot and Pour.

You need a place where you can jot everything and anything down. Notes, scenes, ideas. No censor, no rules and no expectations. Many brilliant thinkers have kept journals (Einstein, da Vinci, Tesla, to name a few). Writing down your thoughts is an important part of the creative process because it creates a feedback loop that keeps the ideas fresh and flowing.

Frequently Asked Questions

Q: I'm on my first draft. How is writing the first draft different from the rest of the writing process?

A: A first draft is a launching point. It's also a mixed bag. The great part? A first draft is something real and tangible. You can hold it in your hands. You can point to it and proudly jump up and down. It's an accomplishment. The less than great part? It's an imperfect accomplishment. The job of the first draft is to be wonderfully raw, unfinished and clunky.

"The first draft of the script or manuscript is something you have to pass through on the way to quality." —John Vorhaus, *The Comic Toolbox: How to Be Funny Even If You're Not*

You may have heard the phrase "writing is rewriting." And that is true. Without that all-important first draft, you can't move forward—you need something to rewrite. The first draft is probably the most important part of the writing process and the place where most writers give up.

Understanding that you are going to create something that is

beautifully imperfect

is essential to first draft success.

Q: What are the 11 Commandments for writing a first draft?

A: So glad you asked. Here they are.

The 11 Commandments for Writing a First Draft

1. **Have realistic expectations.** Understand what a first draft is. It's a skeleton. It's THE FRAME of a house. The wooden beams and concrete floor. No tiled roof or pretty painted windows. Just the basics. If you get any more than that, great. But expect to get the frame of your story and be happy with that, damn it.
2. **Write daily.** Writing daily keeps you in shape, keeps you moving, discovering and working toward your goal. Judy Reeves, the author of *A Writer's Book of Days*, states, "*If you will practice every day, and be gentle with yourself, you will be amazed. Your writing will be fresher, livelier, and more spontaneous. You will take more risks, write more passionately, and reach into places you didn't know existed.*"
3. **Take care of your body and mind.** Do your best to eat well, sleep well, exercise regularly and care for your soul. Caring for your body translates into a more flexible, creative mind.
4. **Don't talk about the project you are working on much (if at all).** I prefer to tell only one or two people because it helps me to remain accountable. Other than that, I keep my mouth shut during the first draft phase. Some writers do not talk about their writing until they have a readable draft. Why? Talking about it seems to take some of the energy out of you that you might use for writing. Also, you risk getting discouraged by somebody's misguided opinions. Think of yourself as entering a nest of creation, and limit the number of opinions that enter this nest.
5. **Keep your muse well fed.** Discover what inspires you and keep it handy. I love to read *The Art of Dramatic Writing* by Lajos Egri and *The Art and Craft of Playwriting* by Jeffrey Hatcher. In my mind, both

are classics, and they always feed me ideas for my writing practice. I also like *Calvin and Hobbes*.

6. **Learn how to manage poisonous thoughts and moods.** The inner critic, self-defeating thoughts, the anti-writer—whatever you call it, every writer experiences thoughts and moods that work against their productivity. Every writer can work through his or her poisonous thoughts differently. But you MUST, I repeat, MUST find out how to manage them. (More on this in Tool #1.)
7. **Commit to finishing.** Use *The Morning Sentence* on Page 40. As you will learn, this tenacious attitude is vital for the entire process.
8. **Incorporate play into your writing routine.** It will make writing the first draft more of a lighthearted adventure. You will beat yourself up less, and your ideas will be fresher and more plentiful.
9. **Expect incompleteness, awkwardness and fat.** A first draft comes out with many holes, with uninspired moments, with sentences that don't make sense and tons of overwriting. Is it still a successful first draft? YES!
10. **Do the prewriting work.** Just do it. You will want to skip the planning and just start putting words on the page. I know you. But don't do it. Make a map first. There is a reason for so much planning. You will thank me when you get to the midpoint, and you are not inexplicably stuck, or when you go to rewrite, and you are not staring at a confusing, jumbled mess of words.
11. **Reward yourself for the small moments.** So many people curtail their writing because "It's just not coming out perfectly brilliant." Learn to reward yourself in small ways for staying committed and focused and for keeping the words flowing. Reward yourself when the words come out crappy and you write the next day anyway!

"Even if you write it wrong, write and finish your first draft. Only then, when you have a flawed whole, do you know what you have to fix."
—Dominick Dunne

Q: What can get in the way of my writing successfully?

A: Stubbornness, Perfectionist Thinking and Overthinking.

Stubbornness

Writers are often stubborn and fiercely independent thinkers. They struggle with being told what to do. I hear ya. I was the same way. I often made things more difficult for myself because I didn't want to hear that there was a way that worked for others (or for thousands of years, for that matter). I had to find my own way. I knew what was best for my writing. That attitude led to a few years of running into walls—until I was open enough to learn from the wisdom of others.

Perfectionist Thinking

Oh, how we all wish we could just magically sit down to write and have all the words flow out in perfect order with perfect clarity and precision.

If you are leaning in this direction at all, you may have a case of perfectionist thinking. In order to cope with the perfectionist bug as quickly and efficiently as possible, it is imperative that you readjust your expectations about writing and learn how to tackle your inner critic.

Bottom line: Embracing imperfection is a key attitude shift for writing success.

"Understand that it always comes out in the end somewhat less ideally than imagined when getting started. Don't expect to be satisfied."
—Richard Walter, *Essentials of Screenwriting*

Overthinking

My best advice is not to overthink the 7 Tools. Overthinking can lead to second-guessing, spinning your wheels, self-doubt and then, ultimately, not moving forward. Your job is to be open enough to try out the tools. If one works for you, you have a tool for life. If it doesn't, modify it or move on and try another. If that aspect of writing is coming to you naturally, then you probably don't need to focus on it (though some writers love to dive into the mechanics because they feel it takes their craft to the next level).

Know that the more you use the 7 Tools, the easier they will become and the stronger you will be as a writer.

I am by no means stating that mastering each tool is easy. To promise that would not make me an effective guide. What I can promise is that if you stick with me—if you stick with your story—you will have completed something so completely satisfying that it almost feels like getting a pat on the back from storytellers of centuries past.

Q: Where do we get our stories, and why are we called to tell them?

A: That I cannot answer definitively. The best answer I can come up with, after doing this for decades, is that it is a combination of mind, mystery and magic. Some writers believe that they may be tapping into a universal story—a story that may rest deep within all of us. Some writers believe they may be tapping into a collective consciousness while others feel they are channeling from an unknown source. Again, I'm not sure. But if you are connected to a story, you are part of a long history of thinkers and dreamers called to tell a tale or impart information from the great beyond and through your fingertips.

Q: Do I need to know the title right away?

A: Nope. You can use a "working title" or wait until the end. It's up to you.

Q: How can I tell if I have a good or not-so-good writing routine?

A:

- Not-So-Good Routine: Your progress is slow or stopped. Your energy is being drained. You are starting to believe your inner critic.
- Good Routine: You are making slow and steady progress. You feel challenged and excited. Your work is feeding your soul. You may hear your inner critic, but you are able to turn it down or tune it out altogether.

(If you find yourself in the not-so-good area, see Writing Tool #1.)

Q: Can the 7 Tools be used for all types of writing?

A: Yes. I am going to include pointers that will assist you with screenplays, plays, novels, short stories and memoirs (although memoirs require some additional tools that I will be exploring in my next book!).

Q: How do I know if I'm a writer?

A: Diagnosis: Writer

- Impatient.
- Filled with self-doubt and occasional self-loathing.
- Has trouble finishing a piece of work.
- Hates their material, especially while writing the middle, end or beginning.

- Considers themselves to have Attention Deficit Disorder → easily distracted.
- Suffers from extreme procrastination.
- Knows that their work will never be "good enough."
- Will often only complete material when there is a concrete deadline.
- Has an internal critic that is so loud it can drown out the creative process.
- Gets best ideas while showering, walking the dog or chopping broccoli.
- Thinks the words must come out perfectly on the page the first time.
- Beats themselves up when the first draft needs work.
- Thinks the next project will be *so* much better.
- Reads other writers and bashes themselves for not being as good as those authors.
- Finds chores, emails to answer or websites to explore instead of writing.
- Dislikes planning and outlining; wants to jump in and get all the words on the page.
- Prone to worry, panic and fear.

Get the picture? Bottom line: We writers are not kind to ourselves.

Infrequently Asked Questions

(Nobody asks me these questions, but they are good ones.)

Q: How do writers learn?

A: Writers learn in layers or stages.

If you wanted to be an artist but had never painted a painting, would you sit down at an easel with your paint and brushes and expect to create a masterful piece of art? No. You'd listen and learn from other artists and eventually go to a class and find a teacher. As you went through training, you would learn in stages: Maybe you'd learn about the color wheel first, then shading, then composition, then depth and space. You might then move on to integrate shadows and highlights, blending and movement. In other words, you'd see it as a process.

For some reason, new writers expect to be able to simply pick up a pen and write a masterpiece. (And they are often very hard on themselves if they don't succeed on the first try.) The truth is that it will take you time, and you will learn in stages. Writers integrate and understand the writing process one concept at a time. For example, a writer may come to understand crafting character first but still struggle with plot, then integrate more skillful dialogue, then subtext, then theme and tone. Here are a few of the layers that writers tend to integrate one at a time:

- Plot
- Character
- Dialogue
- Tone
- Personal Voice

- Theme
- Maximizing the Premise

Q: If I push through the difficult moments when I want to give up on my writing, what awaits me?

A: Magic awaits you. I have noticed that the writers who continue on with their writing journey, who push through the tough parts and do not give up, will reach a magic moment when they can synthesize all the information they have learned and paint that extraordinary and complex work of art. Be patient with yourself. Don't expect to understand all the layers at once. Work with one concept at a time. Work with it until you get it and feel ready to move on. See yourself on a journey to create that work you are incredibly proud of. Just know it takes time, faith and determination.

Q: Can you make it any easier?

A: Yes! Lighten up. It's only words, and we can always rearrange them if we don't like the way they come out. (I've noticed that writers learn more easily by adopting a playful spirit.)

What You Will Need

- Notebook or computer
- Writing tools (pen, pencil, computer)
- Either two documents or two notebooks; one for plotting, one for pouring
- An open mind

Okay. 'Nuff said. You ready for the journey? Let's set out to sea.

(Don't worry, I have the map.)

NOW LET'S GET YOU WRITING!

TOOL #1

Your Tenacious WRITING ROUTINE

What good are tools if you don't sit down to actually write?

"The trick is putting your ass where your heart wants to be." —Steven Pressfield, *The War of Art*

No One Wants to Buy Boy Scout Popcorn

Let me preface this by saying that I was a pretty timid Girl Scout. So I have no idea where my son, Ben, got this from, but this is how it went.

Six years old, first time as a Cub Scout at a seriously crowded street fair. Hundreds of people swarming. Boy Scouts much older than him were nervously hiding behind their parents at the back of the booth.

Let's be clear about one thing. No one wants Boy Scout popcorn. No one. They all want Girl Scout cookies. But no one wants a $10 bag of average Cracker Jack corn (no offense, Boy Scouts). So we sat and watched the thick, menacing Girl-Scout-cookie-loving crowd. That's when my little son piped up. "Um, why is no one asking the people if they want to buy some popcorn?" No one had an answer. Crickets.

Then Ben swiftly picked up a bag and stood in front of an oncoming crowd.

"Excuse me? Anyone want to buy popcorn?" No one did. We knew what was coming next: the slinking back with drooped shoulders to claim defeat. But it didn't happen. He just stood there until another crowd passed by. "Popped corn... anyone?" Nothing.

But the littlest Cub Scout did not budge. He fearlessly, unknowingly stayed the course. We all marveled as he continued to ask whoever passed by. Then, lo and behold, a huge man stopped. (In my mind, he was the size of a bear.) My son gave him the pitch. The bear-sized man pulled out $10 and Ben handed over the bag. We all silently cheered. And Ben kept on like that the whole day. If someone said, "No thanks," he just kept on, until he sold every single bag.

When we got into the car to go home, I asked him how he was able to just keep on like that.

"What do you mean, Mom?"

"I mean, how come you were able to keep going, even when a bunch of people said no?"

He shrugged. "I guess I didn't hear the noes cause I was waiting for the yeses."

There it was—my strongest lesson in tenacity.

Tenacity—It's a Life Shift

I have worked with thousands of writers. Each one thinks he or she is the only one who has difficulty getting words on the page. Why? Because for some reason, we avoid, postpone and curse the very thing we love to do most. We set up impossible expectations. We believe the words must flow out perfectly and succinctly. We think our current idea is not as good as the one bubbling up to the surface. Shiny things distract us. We get to the middle—and sometimes even to the end—and then put our work on a shelf.

Also, today more than ever, our lives require juggling. You may have a day job, kids, a spouse, aging parents, health issues... and the list goes on. For many of the writers I work with, learning to "squeeze in" writing is essential.

No matter what you have filling your life at the moment, by embracing the life of a writer you are making a shift—and this shift requires tenacity.

The most important tool in this book is this one. It teaches you that you are making a life shift, not just a schedule shift.

Shifting to embrace the life of a writer may not be easy. You will probably encounter some resistance. In my work as a therapist with writers and artists, I teach people how to travel through the Phases of Transformation (and I'll teach you, too—stay tuned).

Why Tenacity?

Studying geniuses like Galileo, Mozart, Einstein and Picasso, I learned one thing they all had in common. Besides being smart and creative, they were all crazy tenacious. There was no stopping the train they were on. They were moving.

This is how you want to be. Tenaciously moving, deliciously engaged, no matter what. Sooner or later, the world will catch up with you and acknowledge your presence. But only the tenacious survive long enough to see that happen.

Q: How long do I need to be tenacious?

A: Throughout the five steps of the writing process.

Writing Process

1. Brainstorming

2. Words on the page

3. Editing

4. Polishing

5. Publication and PR (getting the work out there)

Q: What's the healthiest way to be tenacious?

A: You want to be a dancing tortoise. (Stay with me a minute.)

You know the story of the tortoise and the hare, right? (Super-swift hare runs a race against a super-slow tortoise. The hare is fast but is unfocused and overconfident and falls asleep, and the tortoise moves at a slow and steady pace and ends up winning.) Slow and steady really does win the race. So when you hear a lot of hullabaloo about completing something in 30 days or 60 days or anything that tells you that you must run really fast, watch out. Long-term success comes to the tortoise. And why do you want to be a *dancing* tortoise? Slow, steady and enjoying the journey. Best recipe for success ever.

What Kind of Writer Are You?

In some ways, we writers are all alike (the self-doubt, the attention deficit, the procrastination), and in some ways we are ferociously unique. Some writers like to plan their stories out from top to bottom before actually getting words on the page. Some writers like to sit down at the page and allow whatever wants out to come out.

We call these different types of writers "Planners" and "Pantsers."

Planners → Outline their material before writing.

Pantsers → Fly by the seat of their pants.

See if you can identify what kind of writer you are:

1. The Engineer → All Plan, No Pants
2. The Architect → Mostly Plan, Smidge of Pants
3. The Buddha → Half Plan, Half Pants
4. The Intuitive → Mostly Pants, Smidge of Plan
5. The Free Spirit → All Pants, No Plan

I used to be a total Pantser (a Free Spirit) and while it got me a lot of material, it didn't get me very far as a writer. I had to learn to combine the two to create work that had enough structure to be solid craft-wise and enough freedom so that my spirit was in the work. Thus, *plot* and *pour*, or moving back and forth between outlining/brainstorming and free writing, was born. Type #3, or the Buddhas, are the best at plotting and pouring.

I won't lie to you. This book is about gently guiding you to be more like the Buddha type. On the other hand, if the only way you will get material out is to be the Intuitive or the Free Spirit, then get the words out. Get them out however you can. The issue is that the less you plan, the more rewriting you will have to do. You may have to come to terms with losing some of your favorite material if it no longer fits.

If you are a #1 or a #2 ➔ Be open to new ideas coming through during the "words on the page" stage. Writing is a fluid art. Your best-laid plan may not work and, ironically, a better idea might pop up. Be available to listen to the soul of the work.

If you are a #4 or a #5 ➔ Try not to get attached to everything you write. See your first draft as part of the brainstorming stage. Be available to the lesson that your first idea may not be your ultimate and best idea. (Date, but do not marry your ideas yet.)

Uncover Your Creative Process

Each Writer Is a Clock That Ticks in His or Her Own Particular (and Possibly Peculiar) Way

How do you work? How do you come up with ideas? What's the most effective way for you to bring your words to the page? How and when are you the most consistent? What makes you feel inspired? What makes you want to write?

To be tenacious, you need to know the way *your* creative process works.

I started to examine the way I work by studying my morning routine. I'm a kook. In the morning, I dabble from one area of my house to another, getting one thing partially completed, then moving to the next station. I start the coffee, get my son his pants, do a few dishes, then check a few emails, get my son in his shirt and shoes... I found that I get a lot done, but I don't stay on any one task for too long. I dabble in and out. I soon realized that's exactly how I write. I mess around, write, clean out the snack section of the pantry, decide to go gluten-free, write, play with my son, write, decide to go gluten-free tomorrow, weed the garden. You get the picture.

If you don't know your particular creative process → watch yourself. Watch how you do housework, garden, eat, raise a family, fix something, paint, organize work and interact with clients.

Are you highly organized? Do you do one thing at a time? Do you accomplish things in tiny bits? Do you put blinders on and focus like mad?

Do you get lost in your work for long periods of time? Do you have any rituals? What are your wacky habits, your unique patterns?

No matter what your process is, you have one.

How Might You Pick Blackberries?

Prema, one of my talented memoir students, told me about her experience picking blackberries. She said that while everyone else finds an area and pulls the best berries from that spot, she goes from place to place, grabbing some from this spot, some from that spot. She wanders happily, peacefully dabbling from one area to the next.

It's Okay to Get a Little Possessed.

Tenacity requires getting a little possessed. Don't neglect yourself or your loved ones, but feel free to dive into your project and live there for a while. Wake up in the morning with purpose. You are on a mission.

Learn to perform your creative routine without question, over and over, and you will produce results. (This is tenacity.)

Quirky. All of us.

When I sit down to work with a writer (or with a group of writers), we discuss what works for each of them.

What works = what gets a writer to the page consistently, (and in the best cases, playfully).

This is what I have gleaned:

- Writers are quirky nutballs of nuttiness.
- Writers are notoriously self-sabotaging creatures.
- Writers each have their own unique process; they just need to uncover it.

Some examples

1. Jack Kerouac liked to write on scrolls: Pages taped together to form one very long strip of paper.

2. Truman Capote would absolutely never begin a piece of work on a Friday.

3. Wallace Stevens wrote on slips of paper while walking (seeing it as a creative stimulant).

4. Charles Dickens liked to write in blue ink (it dried the fastest).

5. Lewis Carroll preferred purple ink.

6. James Joyce wrote while in bed lying on his stomach, utilizing a crayon or a large blue pencil.

Here are some of the statements that have come out of discussions with writers:

"I can only write after 11 p.m. and only if CNN is on, but not too loud."

"I can write in the morning but only if I'm drinking out of my favorite blue mug."

"I write best in coffee shops that are really busy late at night."

"I write best in empty coffee shops with no music."

7 ESSENTIAL WRITING TOOLS

"If I start to write, I need to have at least two hours of total quiet."

"My best sessions are when I start out using an online brainstorming tool, then move on to my novel."

"I listen to the same music over and over when I'm writing a certain character."

"I tell myself I only have to write for 10 minutes a day just to trick myself into sitting down at all."

"I write best at work, during really boring meetings when I pretend to be listening."

"My best ideas come when I am showering or walking my dog."

"I tell myself I will write one page of crap per day."

"I need to stare out the window, preferably at the rain, for at least 30 minutes before I sit down to write."

"I tell myself all I have to do is read the last scene I wrote to get myself going. Inevitably that gets me interested in my work and I will write something new."

How to Investigate Your Best Writing Habits and Make Them Stick

To create an effective writing routine, you need to know a few things:

1. **When do you write best?** What time of day are you most creative? Early morning, lunchtime, mid-afternoon, late night? (Or are you a dabbler, like me?)

2. **Where do you write best?** Do you write better all alone, in a coffee shop, in nature or at home? Writers can, and do, have several writing spaces. Often, they have their "home base" and their "on-the-go" site. I love my laptop. I write at home with a TV show on and at a kids' cafe while my son runs around in a Spider-Man costume (this is where I am right now). I often want to write in bed, but if I do so, it all goes south. Naps seem inevitable. I have a short time to get this book out and no time to waste on a nap.

3. **How do you write best?** Do you write best with no noise, with your favorite music or in a quiet room with other writers? Do you write best when you have meditated first, lit a candle or talked to your muse? Or is it best to just jump in and go? Do you work well writing in longhand in a spiral notebook or on a laptop or PC? Do you work well with writing software? (Scrivener is a cool one.)

4. **What kind of deadline works for you?** Do you need to break things up in really small chunks: daily or weekly goals? Or do

larger chunks work better: one-month, three-month or six-month goals?

5. **Do you work well with accountability?** If so, what kind of accountability works best? A writing friend, a writing coach, a writing group, a writing calendar, a class or a combination of these elements? Have you looked into accountability groups or apps?

6. **Do you work well with a reward system?** If so, do you need small rewards for daily work or larger rewards for monthly work? One of my awesome students, Maria, came up with a system wherein every time she completes a goal, she puts a little money in a "writing fund." At the end of the year, she takes a cool trip to a writing retreat or goes to a fun writing conference she's always wanted to attend.

7. **Do you have a regular play routine?** What is something that you do for fun that promotes spontaneous thought, brainstorming and fresh ideas?

8. **How can you "squeeze in" writing if you already have a full life?** With everything else that you are undoubtedly juggling, when can you make room for your writing practice: breaks, after the kids are asleep, before anyone wakes up, on the weekends? I work with writers who have serious family and work demands, yet they still want to pursue their dreams. You may need to reprioritize your day and eliminate some part of your routine that you truly don't need. Or you may want to create a new habit such as getting up an hour earlier, writing at lunchtime or creating a quiet space for yourself when everyone is in bed. Reminder apps help to keep those that love technology on task. What I have found, though, is that even the most time-challenged person—if willing—can find pockets of time.

If you need a good, solid routine, I suggest you do two things:

- Pay attention to how you get things done.

- Take a week or two to experiment. Test out coffee shops, noise levels, software, surroundings, routines and rituals. Make notes. Then…

Whatever works, do more of it.

If it doesn't work, toss it.

Incorporate Play Into Your Writing Routine

"Find your 'Heart Play' and everything else you want in life will come along." —Barbara Brannen, *The Gift of Play: Why Adult Women Stop Playing and How to Start Again*

We will cover this more deeply in Tool #7 (Voice) but let me just plant a few notions in your noggin.

Adding play into your writing routine will

- Promote a healthy flow of fresh, unique ideas (otherwise known as brainstorming).
- Help to squash the inner critic.
- Encourage the all-important tenacious attitude.
- Make the process a whole heck of a lot more fun.

Play can include running, painting, sailing, crossword puzzles, dancing, singing, gaming, nature walks, going to the zoo, hanging out with a child or pet, collaging, knitting, scrapbooking, taking pictures, scuba diving, snorkeling, surfing, whale watching (strike that, it's nauseating), meditative walking, baking, filming, editing, inventing, directing, laughing with friends, playing sports, brainstorming with other writers… and on and on. Add a dash of play to your writing to keep it lively and flowing.

 Hint: Try to add something that will be complementary to your life. For example: If you are fairly sedentary, try to incorporate play with movement. (You'd be surprised how many writers report that their best ideas arrive while walking the dog.)

Incorporate Positive Thinking Into Your Routine

We all live with the noise of the inner critic.

If you can lessen the noise, do it.

There are ways to lessen your lousy thoughts—and thereby tame your inner critic a bit. I've heard many success stories about people who retrained their brain to think more positively.

Here's an excellent tool for keeping the inner critic in check. Simply counter the negative thought with an equally opposing positive thought.

Common inner critic thoughts: Who am I to write? This is going all wrong. I have another idea that's much better. This sucks. I can't do this. Who will want to read what I have to say? I'm out of ideas. I'm overwhelmed.

Here are the countering positive thoughts:

Old Thought →	Change to →	New Thought
Who am I to write?	→	What I have to say is valid and important.
This is going all wrong.	→	Writing is filled with ups and downs. An up is coming.
I have another idea that's much better.	→	This idea is worth finishing. Perfection is not required.
This sucks.	→	I'm hitting a rough patch, and I can get through it.
I can't do this.	→	I can do this.
Who will want to read what I have to say?	→	My work will find its perfect audience.
I'm out of ideas.	→	The perfect idea is coming to me.
I'm overwhelmed.	→	Step by step, slow and steady wins the race. (Think dancing tortoise.)

In other words, you need to learn how to talk yourself down from the ledge. Start by acknowledging that this is your inner critic talking and not "THE TRUTH." Don't believe everything you think. Then, walk yourself through the primary negative thought. Fight back; don't buy the inner critic's take on things.

Q: What if my inner critic doesn't listen to my new thoughts?

A: You can spend time fighting it. You can work with cognitive behavioral tools to help you change your poisonous thoughts and moods. It's all good. But, if you have tried that (let's just say you have tried all that), and you're still sabotaging yourself: then what?

Use the Phases of Transformation. Pay special attention to Step #3 (Grab Your Shadow; It's Coming With You).

USE THE NEXT SECTION IF

- You want your new changes to stick.
- You have difficulty staying on task.
- You want to fully embrace the writer's life.
- You want to understand how real transformation happens.
- You have difficulty making space in your life for writing.
- You tend to sabotage your writing practice.
- You struggle with anxiety or fear-based thinking.

WANT TO MAKE SURE YOUR NEW HABITS WILL STICK?

→ Follow the...

Phases of Transformation

Just so you know: You can use this recipe for any change you'd like to make in your life.

Today, we are going to help you to fully embrace your life as a writer.

These steps will help you to stay committed and focused (for longer and longer periods of time) until you have changed your habits and embraced your writer's life:

1. Pick a writing goal
2. Make space
3. Grab your shadow; it's coming with you
4. Enter the discomfort
5. Allow and applaud the transformation

Let's walk through it, and I will show you how it works. (It's really pretty simple.)

1. PICK A WRITING GOAL

This can be anything from creating a writing routine, completing a first draft, completing an outline, polishing your 12th draft, finding an agent, etc.

In my experience, it's best not to mess around here. Don't dilly or dally. Pick a clean and clear goal. Say it out loud or write it down. You know what you want even if you hide it from yourself from time to time.

Grab a notebook. Finish this sentence without censoring yourself at all:

What I want to do is _____.

If your response is, "I don't know," then take a guess. If you still don't know, take a wild, crazy, you-can-totally-be-wrong guess. (Nine times out of ten, a writer will spit something out and whatever they say is usually a great place to start.)

2. MAKE SPACE

Making space involves creating both physical and spiritual space. Of course, you need the physical time and space to work. You may also need to ask for assistance (from the universe) for the spiritual space. You can ask for assistance by praying or meditating; just do whatever you do to connect. This is an especially important tool for writers who struggle to allow writing into their life on a regular basis. Ask for the space to be made available so that your goal can become a reality.

Physical Space

- Get up early or stay up late.
- Keep a small notebook with you at all times.

- Write on small breaks.
- Use a voice recorder.
- Ask family/friends for some childfree time or hire a babysitter.
- Kick-start your writing practice with a writers' retreat. Find one or create one.
- Grab a few friends, rent a house or grab a tent and go camping for the weekend.
- Ask friends or relatives for help.
- Join a writers' group.
- Learn about time management for the writer. (See Appendix 1, page 305)

Spiritual Space

- Pray, ask the universe for the time and space.
- Meditate.
- Exercise.
- Go out into nature.
- Call upon your muses.
- Ask for courage, a push or inspiration—ask for what you need.

3. GRAB YOUR SHADOW; It's Coming with You

What's my shadow and why is it coming?

Shadow: anxiety, worry, panic, fear, shame, self-sabotage, self-doubt, inner critic.

And why is it coming, again?

Two reasons

- There's a chance that if you grab your shadow side and pull it into the light, it will lessen its negative impact on your life.

- You want to be "in movement" as much as possible. Remember that this movement doesn't have to be fast and furious; in fact, it can be slow and steady (think dancing tortoise). So if your inner critic won't budge, so be it. Most writers I know are stuck with some form of lousy thinking—and lousy thinking should not deter you from making progress.

So, grab your shadow and get going.

Bottom line: It may be there, but it's not going to stop you from writing.

4. ENTER THE DISCOMFORT

Even though you are doing something positive for yourself, it may feel uncomfortable.

Even though it may feel uncomfortable, you are heading in the right direction.

Feeling uncomfortable is actually a good sign. (I know, weird huh?)

The good news: You will feel more comfortable with time as you transform your habits.

Q: While I'm in this place of discomfort, is there anything I can do to feel better?

A: Yep, it's called self-care.

SELF-CARE
Eat Well, Sleep Well, Exercise, Rest, Relax

I can tell you want to skip this part of the book but don't. Yes, that means you.

"If you tell me to take care of myself, I'm walking out of here."

This is what I said to the therapist who was trying to help me through a difficult time. I have a low tolerance for people telling me about self-care. Eat broccoli, sleep eight hours a night, nurture your soul and all that psychobabble crap. So why am I pushing it on you?

Two reasons

- Well… 'cause it works. You are your only caretaker. No one else can do it. (And broccoli is good for you.)
- Writers sometimes forget that they live in a body. They spend so much time in their heads, in a bubble of their own imagining, that they forget the basics.

So please don't close the book or throw it across the room (just yet). As annoying as it is, **taking care of your body will make you a calmer, happier, more efficient writing machine.**

Feed Your Brain. To put it simply, for your brain to function properly, you need to feed your body the right amounts of protein and nutrients. Feeding your body the right foods will help you in boosting memory, mood, mental endurance, focus and overall ability to be creative.

Shut Those Eyes. If you don't sleep, you may run the risk of experiencing:

- Difficulty paying attention or staying on task.
- Difficulty making decisions or remembering what you wanted to say.
- Irritability and low mood (which may appear to you as lack of excitement about your work that day).
- Muddled or "less clear" thinking.
- Slowing down your ability to think up new ideas.

Furthermore, being able to dream has been said to be very important to the creative process:

- Robert Louis Stevenson came up with the plot of *The Strange Case of Dr. Jekyll and Mr. Hyde* during a dream.
- Paul McCartney discovered the tune for the song "Yesterday" in a dream and was inspired to write "Yellow Submarine" during hypnagogia (the state between sleeping and wakefulness).
- Mary Wollstonecraft Shelley's *Frankenstein* was inspired by a dream at Lord Byron's villa.
- Otto Loewi, a German physiologist, won the Nobel Prize for medicine in 1936 for his work on the chemical transmission of nerve impulses. He discovered in a dream how to prove his theory.

Move That Body. Dr. John J. Medina, a developmental molecular biologist and author of the *New York Times* bestseller *Brain Rules: 12 Principles for Surviving and Thriving at Work, Home, and School*, states that exercise improves cognition for two reasons:

- Exercise increases oxygen flow into the brain, which reduces brain-bound free radicals. Oxygen is always accompanied by an uptick in mental sharpness.
- Exercise acts directly on the molecular machinery of the brain itself. It increases neurons' creation, survival and resistance to damage and stress.

Find Your Inner Kid and Skip Down the Block:

Play! Besides everything else we have covered, play and/or relaxation help to nurture your mental health. So don't take yourself too seriously. Take small breaks. Exhale. When you return to your work, you will be fresh.

To recap: So far you have picked a goal, made space, grabbed your shadow, entered the discomfort and learned to take care of yourself along the way. What's next?

5. ALLOW AND APPLAUD THE TRANSFORMATION

In this phase, you kinda want to turn off your brain and move your fingers. (It tends to get in the way.)

You'll want to put yourself into the **Horse-race Mindset:**

- Put your blinders on. Run your own race. Forget about what anyone else is doing.

Some people call it brain dumping. Whatever you call it, *stay in movement.*

That's right: Stop thinking so much!

To Move, You Have to Show Up. So Just Show Up:

Forget about timing. You don't need to get it all done in 30 days or whatever crap you've heard. The finish line will come when it comes. It's showing up as often as possible that keeps you where you want to be—on the path.

> **Applaud the Small Victories:**
>
> You will transform. It happens slowly, but it happens. Do your best in this phase to NOTICE THE SMALL MOMENTS OF PROGRESS. Notice and then pat yourself on the back.
>
> Small movements are important movements.
>
> Your goal here is to work smarter and more diligently for longer and longer periods of time. Maybe the first month, you could only wrangle yourself to write for two days a week. Applaud that. See that as evidence that you can do this writing thing. Then next month, you may find that you can write for three days a week. If you find your shadow taking over, go back to Step #2 and make space or ask for help.

What It Looks Like When You Fight Your Transformation:

A writer who had broken through four years of writers block once told me: "Okay, so I wrote for three days straight. Big deal. It was only three days."

What It Looks Like When You Allow the Transformation:

Once this writer learned the Phases of Transformation and, specifically, how to applaud the transformation, he began to say things like: "I know it's just half a chapter, but I think this is proof I can do this."

You will transform.

Notice it.

Applaud it.

Then move some more.

(You can stay in the "allow and applaud the transformation" phase for a while.)

Madonna and Miguel → Two Writers Reveal How They Used the Phases of Transformation

Madonna's Story

Madonna had always wanted to be a writer, but she felt overwhelmed by her life's responsibilities. She was a mom with two kids, and she had a husband, a sick mother and a truly demanding career as an ER nurse. She figured she'd never find the time to write. She kept track of her progress through the Phases of Transformation for eight months.

Example: #1 — Madonna: Create a Writing Routine

- → **Pick a writing goal** → *My goal is to create a writing routine that will stick.*
- → **Make space** → *I did all the things I was supposed to do. I asked for help; I found moments in my day where I could sneak in writing and I even turned down a volunteer position I'd normally take. But none of that worked really well. If I had the time, I'd fill it up with everything on my have-to-do-first list. Then I started to pray. I called on Jesus a few times and Buddha once or twice. I prayed and prayed for God to allow me the space. I took a few personal days and got myself started.*
- → **Grab your shadow** → *I suffer from extreme procrastination. I think that writing is the last thing I should do since I have so many real responsibilities. And I also fear that what I have to say*

will never be good enough. But I'm miserable when I don't write. Some part of me just knows that I should be writing. So I decided that procrastination and fear will come with me on the journey but will not stop me. It might be baggage I have to lug around, but I was okay with it.

→ **Enter the discomfort** → *As I experimented with new times and places, I found I wrote best in the morning, at a coffee shop, in a notebook with a good pen, with the phone turned off. I was having some success, but I felt guilty for not doing more productive work. It felt comfortable to write—but what was uncomfortable was <u>allowing</u> myself the time to write. Nothing helped. I sat with the discomfort. I figured it was more of my baggage coming along.*

→ **Allow and applaud the moments of transformation** → *Any work I did at the coffee shop, I would put on my desk at work and look at it for the rest of the day. I just put my little spiral notebook somewhere I could see it. As I walked by, I was reminded that I had written that day. Sometimes I went back to praying for space. Somehow this just made me beat myself up less. It was like God was part of my plan now—so how could it be a bad plan? I became a regular at the coffee shop in the morning. I filled notebooks. I was a little impatient because I really wanted to start learning French, but I knew I shouldn't distract myself. I pushed myself to stick to my original goal. Six months into the routine, I began to notice when I was moving in and out of my "best writing routine." Overall, when I looked back, I had stuck to the routine. I was halfway through a first draft. I had to pray and kick my shadow around many, many times (more times than I would have liked). But somewhere in those months, writing this damn thing just became a part of my life. Proof positive came the other day—I had to fill out a form, and in the spot where it said occupation, instead of putting "nurse" I put "writer."*

Miguel's Story

Miguel had studied writing for three years. He was filled with ideas for science fiction novels. The problem was that every time he got halfway through a novel, he would quit. He felt that he was a novice and that any new idea was probably better than his original idea. Then he saw that he was sabotaging himself. He followed the Phases of Transformation, and this is what he reported.

Example #2 — Miguel: Finish the First Draft of My Novel

- **Pick a writing goal** → *My goal was to finish the first draft of my novel. This novel, not a new one. <u>This</u> novel.*
- **Make space** → *I used meditation when I asked for the space. I took one less client on at work and lived a bit more on the cheap. I also added visualization. Three minutes a day I visualized my completed manuscript. I found out that I work best midday, in between clients, on my laptop in a conference room or an empty office.*
- **Grab your shadow** → *I once had a therapist tell me I suffered from Generalized Anxiety Disorder (GAD). I always thought that was a terrible thing to tell someone. Then I realized that my anxiety was blocking my ability to finish a novel. I decided that I might have GAD—as she called it—but so what. GAD and I would write a novel.*
- **Enter the discomfort** → *I suck at self-care. As I pushed myself to write daily, I noticed how uncomfortable it felt. The anxiety took over sometimes and I found myself worrying about the craziest stuff instead of writing. I remembered that I was supposed to feel uncomfortable, and it made me feel a little better. But not much.*

- **Allow and applaud the moments of transformation** → *I realized I was experiencing a lot of anxiety as I was hitting the middle. I had never gotten past the middle. Every page I wrote that pushed me past the middle, I swear I did a victory dance—like a touchdown-kinda-victory dance. Once I finished the dreaded middle section, I just became a monster. In a good way. I was almost so determined to finish that I forgot to take care of myself. The anxiety was somehow way down for a few months. I had a bad time for a few weeks when life got hectic, but I fought my way back. It's crazy now because when I go to tell people about the book, I'm still amazed that I wrote a book. At times, I was a ball of anxiety. But somehow it worked; I mean it must have because I actually wrote a book.*

What If, What If, What If?

Q: You work on so many things, how do you do it all?

A: People ask me this all the time. The answer is that I have a severe case of Attention Deficit Disorder (ADD: self-diagnosed). I am extremely distracted by shiny things. I wake up all excited and determined to write a children's story about a wacky goose learning to ride a tricycle, but by midday I think my time would be better spent on a self-help book about the power of surrender, and then by night I've chucked both ideas. Sound familiar?

What if my problem is that I get distracted easily?

Or... *How to Demand Focus in Our Attention-Deficit World:*

Our attention is being pulled in so many directions in today's world that sometimes it's hard to know how to focus or what to focus on. Last night, I was watching TV when the host promoted what he called a "three-screen experience." I'm assuming that one was the TV; the other was a laptop and the third a phone so that you could be interacting online or tweeting your thoughts on the show in real time.

Now, I'm the queen of multitasking, but this seemed extreme even to me. Why, oh why, are we *always* multitasking? And how does multitasking impact a writing routine?

Writing requires space, time—and often quiet. Our world is getting faster and louder. And it's not going to calm down anytime soon. The next few decades will be even faster and louder than the last. So the writer must absolutely demand time and space to write.

Carve out time with no Facebook or tweeting or texting or phone or emails or tablets. Just you and your thoughts.

Simple and clean rule for the writer: Reject faster and louder while you are writing. Nurture your inner dancing tortoise (slow and steady). Nurture calm. Nurture just that moment for being just that moment.

What if I'm lacking inspiration?

Sometimes, in the middle of the work, you may find that you feel less than enthused. That's the time that you want to light your work on fire. The ideas are not flowing. The inspiration has dissipated. If and when you find yourself in this predicament, check this out:

Inspiration Scale—How inspired do you feel currently about your project?

10 - Completely inspired
9 - Almost completely inspired
8 - Mostly inspired
7 - Occasional bouts of feeling uninspired
6 - Feeling uninspired often
5 - Half the time I feel inspired, half the time I don't
4 - Often feeling uninspired
3 - Rarely feeling inspired
2 - Almost completely out of inspiration
1 - What is inspiration?

Score_____

If you scored anything below a 5, go to →

Ideas to Up Your Inspiration

Go to the bookstore or library. Pick up a book. Allow the thoughts of other writers to dance inside you a little bit. Take yourself on a field trip. Research your topic. Learn a new method to access your creativity (meditation, etc.). Take a new creative class (drawing, sculpture, clay, etc.). Walk, exercise, spend time with a mountain. See a play or movie; let a good storyteller talk to you. Combine ordinary things in extraordinary ways. Look at ordinary things with extraordinary eyes. Have lunch with the most prolific or creative person you know. Collage your ideas; let the images come to you. Pay attention to all the senses: smell, sight, sound, touch and taste. Look at your writing from a child's perspective. Read visual writers. Think of putting two different ideas together. Listen to music. Read books—all kinds. Poetry. Plays. Movies. Memoirs. Short Stories.

Understanding Resistance

The bigger the dream, the bigger the resistance. They are like yin and yang. With one comes the other. So just acknowledge the resistance and move on.

Fear is part of the game. It's normal. Do it anyway.

Q: What if my commitment starts waning?

A: The goal here is to have 100 percent commitment to finishing a first draft. But chances are that from time to time, your commitment may fluctuate.

COMMITMENT CHECK—Where are you on the commitment scale?

- 10 - Completely committed
- 9 - Highly committed
- 8 - Very committed with small doubts
- 7 - Occasional doubts but still strongly committed
- 6 - Still mostly committed with more frequent doubts
- 5 - Half the time I feel committed, half the time I don't
- 4 - Losing steam
- 3 - Only occasional bouts of determination, mostly discouraged
- 2 - Almost ready to quit
- 1 - I quit

Score_____

If you scored anything below a 5, go to →

IDEAS TO MAINTAIN COMMITMENT

- Get an accountability partner.
- Offer yourself clear rewards for small goals.
- Use writing software that helps keep you on task.
- Keep an inspiring writing book on hand. Read morning or night.
- Join a writing group.
- Write yourself a commitment letter with a strong affirmation.
- Find or go to your writing cheerleader—you know the person. The "you-can-do-it-no-matter-what!" person.
- Take a step back and applaud yourself for what you have already accomplished. Before, there was nothing; now there is something.
- Set up a target date—like a contest you will submit your work to (or a fellowship or grant, etc.).
- Spruce up your writing routine by adding a ritual such as music, lighting a candle, making your favorite coffee or tea.
- Hire a cool writing coach.
- Think of what has worked for you in the past: a group, an encouraging word, a bribe, a deadline? Chances are, if it worked for you in one field, it could work for you here as well.

Keeping your inspiration up will assist you greatly in keeping up your commitment level.

Q: What is the most effective tool to get writers to the page?

A: When they allow themselves to write crap.

Q: What if my attitude is lousy and I really want to change it?

A: Focus on two attitude adjusters:

1. Every morning when you wake up, commit to finishing *The Morning Sentence*.
2. Become a solution-focused writer.

"Most of the shadows of this life are caused by standing in one's own sunshine." —Ralph Waldo Emerson

How to Do The Morning Sentence

Wake up and say one of these sentences.

If super positivity works for you: *"Today is filled with writing magic and I'm 100 percent committed to finishing."*

If you struggle more with you inner critic: *"I'm not sure how I will get it all done, but I'm 100 percent committed to finishing."*

(You can also create your own *Morning Sentence*.) Making this commitment is vital because there isn't one writer I have ever worked with—ever—who hasn't encountered a moment where they wanted to quit their current project and move on to the next one or just quit writing altogether. You will need this level of commitment to get you through the rough patches.

Here's How to Become a Solution-Focused Writer:

> **Once you find what works for you: DO MORE OF IT!**
> **If it's not working for you, try something different.**

Whenever you encounter a problem—and you will encounter many—embrace the attitude that there is a solution. You are simply on a journey to find it.

Q: What if nothing else works? What if I can't move forward no matter what I try?

A: The best solution I have found for writers who struggle the most is to join a weekly writing group. (Any writing group is great, but weekly is the best.) I have run writing groups for years, and after a few months I notice a shift in the group members. A community is created. Social pressure (in the best way) is working its magic. Commitment is solidified within the writer. They have made an agreement with themselves that "Yes, I am indeed a writer."

Writing groups give the writer a chance to test out material and to take risks. They offer a time to learn craft and uncover your writing voice. But mostly, they nurture the regular habit of writing. Sometimes the only answer is to let a solid, consistent writing community lift you up.

Your Tenacious Writing Routine

What kind of writer am I? _____

My creative process looks like this _____
_____

Where I work best (place) _____

When I work best (time of day) _____

How I work best (method) _____

I am going to work on taking care of myself better by _____
_____
_____

I will incorporate play into my writing routine by _____
_____

My reward system looks like _____
_____

I see myself as tenacious because _____
_____

If I work best on a deadline, here are my goals for:
3 months _____
6 months _____
9 months _____
1 year _____

Takeaway Lessons for Tool #1 Your Tenacious WRITING ROUTINE

- Experiment with time, place and method until you can fill out "Your Tenacious WRITING ROUTINE" worksheet.
- Know that everyone has a creative process. You may need to discover and uncover yours.
- Understand that as you take on a writing practice, you are traveling through natural Phases of Transformation.
- Just show up.
- Demand quiet, calm and time to focus in our attention-deficit world.
- Be a solution-focused writer. Once you find what works: DO MORE OF IT!

So, armed with your TENACIOUS writing routine, are you ready to hone your kick-ass idea? Let's go!

TOOL #2
Creating a Solid STORY IDEA

A solid story idea is one that can be expressed in one to three sentences. The reader can easily understand whom the story is about and the central conflict the protagonist is facing.

A soggy story idea is one where the protagonist is not clearly defined, there is no clear-cut goal or forward-moving action, the theme is unclear, the stakes are low and the conflict is hard to understand.

The Drunk Man Has a Point

One night during one of my writing classes, a student showed up drunk. (It actually took the whole class for me to figure out that he was drunk, but he was cantankerous and opinionated all night.) The topic of the class was about clarifying and honing your core story idea.

I turned to my class and asked them a question:

"Do you know why you are writing about your topic—I mean, do you really know what it is that you want to say?"

Drunk guy stood up and balked. "Why do I have to know everything right away? Can't I just keep writing and I'll find out?"

"Yes," I answered. "You have a point. You can write to find it."

"So, why do you keep making me think so much now?"

"To save you two years of rewriting."

Here's the deal. I talk to a lot of agents, editors, writing teachers and coaches. When discussing new manuscripts, there is one issue that they express frustration about over and over again.

What is it?

They can't follow the story.

Think about that. An agent or an editor sits down to read a manuscript that a writer has been working on for two or three years and what are they thinking?

I wish I could follow this story.

Why is convoluted, unclear writing so common?

Well, while there is no one main reason, there are some common mistakes. Many times, writers stuff too many storylines into the plot, or they try to tell the story from too many points of view, or they shove every idea they have ever had into one plotline. In my experience, the problem is that the writer hasn't ever fully thought through their core idea.

Q: What's the solution?

A: Take your time to craft a solid story idea. (Thinking it through is really not that hard at all. I promise.)

The Core Story Idea: Who, What, Where, When and How. *The protagonist encounters a problem and goes off on a journey and ends up...* The story idea sums up the overall idea in a sentence or two.

Theme: Unifying Message/Central Idea

Plot: How you execute your story idea and theme. The step-by-step movements of the story, the unfolding of events. For now we will set aside plot, as you will be crafting your plot in Tool #4.

Trust me on this one. Your core idea is something you will live with for years. Don't shortchange the process of clarifying it. The stronger it grows in your head before you write it, the stronger it will be on the page.

As discussed before, most beginning writers love the excitement of getting words on the page. The problem comes when they reach the midpoint of their story and are unsure how to keep the conflict going—or worse—finish it only to realize that there are tons of holes throughout the storyline *and* that most of it needs a big old fat rewrite.

Ever been to a writers' conference? If so, you've probably heard a conversation that sounded dangerously close to this one:

> Scott: So what are you working on?
>
> Donna: A book. It's my first novel.
>
> Scott: What's it about?
>
> Donna: Oh, it's kind of hard to explain. It's sort of about England in the 1970s, but also it's from two points of view, Jake and Fiona, and Jake wants to be a rock star,

well, he was a rock star for a little bit, but he has this problem because he's really shy, because he got into this really bad accident and almost died when he was a kid, but the story is really about love, he has never in his life experienced love until he meets this girl Fiona—they have a chance, but there are two problems, he's too shy to say how he feels, and she thinks she's in love with Rick, but mostly, I want to explore how people try to find meaning, and when they don't find meaning it's difficult, and it also has a mystery aspect in there and the other point of view from Fiona. Oh, and Rick is married, and he's her boss, and Fiona wants to be a nurse, oh, and I also talk about the medical system in England, and also Rick is Jake's best friend, and Jake stumbles into a big musical hit on the pop chart and he becomes like crazy famous, but it's really this love triangle.

How might you respond if you heard this story idea? Be honest. Your eyes might glaze over, you might search for comprehension and you might start to tune Donna out completely.

When a writer rambles, what is communicated? → The writer does not truly have control over his or her material.

Q: So how do I create a solid story idea?

A: Well, it's all about five tiny little questions.

> **WHO → PROBLEM → GOAL → STAKES → ENDING**

Creating the Strongest Story Idea Possible

At this moment, you may have a fully fleshed-out idea, or you may have just the kernel of an idea. Either way, answering the following questions will help you hit the target, so to speak.

> A SOLID story idea can identify these five elements swiftly and cleanly.
>
> A SOGGY story idea wanders and cannot answer all five elements.

- **WHO** are you writing about? (Can be a person, family or ensemble of characters.)
- What **PROBLEM** does this person/group face?
- What is the **GOAL** of this person/group?
- What are the **STAKES**? Are the stakes high enough to sustain an entire story?
- How does the person's/group's journey **END**?

Optional but important last question: Of these five elements, which one is unique or bold?

Let's look at Donna's story once more, only let's think it through. (This is the same idea, just presented in a different way.)

Who: Jake, a desperately shy aspiring rock star in 1970s England.

Problem: Hopelessly in love with Fiona, but is too afraid to tell Fiona how he feels. Because he says nothing, Fiona stays with her married lover, Rick.

Goal: Get over his shyness and win Fiona's love.

Stakes: His broken heart and their future happiness.

End: He becomes one of the biggest rock stars in England but never gets the courage to tell Fiona how he feels until it is too late.

Now that Donna has thought it through, when she is telling her story to others it may sound more like this:

Donna: I'm writing a story about Jake, a hopelessly shy aspiring rock star in 1970s England. Jake falls madly in love with Fiona, a nurse he meets on a train. They share a brief romantic encounter, but Jake is too scared to tell Fiona how he feels, and she remains in a relationship with her married boss, Rick. It's a funny and tragic love triangle that follows Jake's search for love as he unwittingly rises to spectacular fame.

Or, if Donna wanted to make the pitch super short, she could trim it down:

It's a funny and tragic love triangle that follows a hopelessly shy rock star's search for love as he unwittingly rises to spectacular fame in 1970s England.

Now we can follow the story. We know we are focusing on what Jake wants (Fiona) and what is at stake if he doesn't get it (a broken heart).

It sounds easy to do, but approximately 85 percent of the writers I work with can greatly improve their idea by asking the five simple story idea questions.

Q: Where do most writers go wrong? (Pay attention to this part.)

A: Two areas

1. The goal is not clear or specific enough.

2. The stakes are just way too low.

I once saw an agent walking around a writer's conference wearing a shirt that read, **"Make Me Care."** At first I saw this as sort of obnoxious, but after eight hours of listening to pitches, I was dazed. Writer after writer had shared their stories in pitch sessions and classes, and none of them was compelling. None had enough bite to capture my imagination. The goals were fuzzy and the stakes were low. By the end of day two I wanted to scream: *Please make me care. Do something, anything.*

By making the goal clear (specific) and raising the stakes, I've seen writers take average pieces of work and make them brilliant, intense and compelling (in other words, they made us care).

Watch out for wishy-washy goals like:

- Get love
- Be a success
- Win self-respect

Those are good places to start. But don't land there. Keep going.

Make it specific.

Q: How, how and how?

A: It's easy peasy. Just add the word *"by"* to the sentence.

Get love *by*: Winning the love of his next-door neighbor, Patricia.

Be a success *by:* Getting his boss's job.

Win self-respect *by*: Completing the race no matter whether she wins.

And...

Remember, successfully reaching the goal can't be easy. Getting Patricia's love, the boss's job or winning the race must be hard. There must be obstacles and an antagonist or two. Once you know your specific goal, ask yourself:

How can I raise the stakes?

In other words, how can I make it hard to win Patricia's love? What are the obstacles in the way? What person is in the way? What circumstances are in the way?

And for those who want to get really geeky:

List all the obstacles that can get in the way of your protagonist getting what they want in order of lowest to highest stakes so your protagonist has to put themselves at increasing peril to achieve their goal.

Example: Brian wants to win Patricia's love.

Off the top of my head, here's what could get in the way of their love:

- Brian doesn't know how to talk to girls.
- Patricia is very preoccupied with her dream to become an Olympic skater.
- Another neighbor boy is wooing Patricia.
- Brian's mother wants Brian to end up with a girl from church.
- Patricia's family might move away.

Brian must overcome one obstacle after another until he reaches the hardest obstacle. Then he either gets his goal or doesn't (depending on if you are writing a tragedy).

Important Note About Comedies

Often in comedies, the protagonist's goal comes with *low* stakes. That is perfectly fine and often works to create more humor. The key is how badly the protagonist WANTS that goal. Look at *The Big Lebowski* (goal is to get his rug back) or *Harold & Kumar Go to White Castle* (goal is to make it to White Castle). What makes these comedies funny is how seriously the leads take their mission. Many of *Seinfeld's* episodes were born of the humor of low stakes but high desire. (I know it's a little old-timey, but did you see the one where Jerry absolutely must have and eventually steals a marble rye bread?)

Sometimes comedies do/can have real stakes. In *Bridesmaids*, the protagonist is in danger of losing her best (and maybe only real) friendship. In *The Grand Budapest Hotel*, a concierge will be charged with murder unless he proves his innocence. In *The Hangover*, they have lost their best friend and groom, and if they can't find him, there will be no wedding (plus, they lost their best friend).

A Brief Case Study on Being Formulaic

Q: Won't reducing my story to five questions make my story formulaic and predictable? (It's a question I get asked often.)

A: Not at all. Let's take a look at one recent success that will diffuse that argument swiftly. *Birdman: Or The Unexpected Virtue of Ignorance*. It won Oscars for Best Picture, Director, Cinematography and Screenplay. It's a story about a washed-up, middle-aged film actor who once played a very popular film superhero called Birdman. The moment we meet him, he is trying to resurrect his career by writing, starring in and directing his first Broadway play. He happens to hear the voice of Birdman (his old character) and is seemingly able to float in air, move objects through sheer will and fly through space. He comes up against an egotistical co-star, troubling familial relationships and an impossible theater critic who is bent on destroying the play. It has an interesting ending that got people talking. And no one could call it predictable. In fact, critics have called it "unique," "different and surreal," "mystical" and a movie that "soars above the Hollywood formula."

But does it have a strong core idea? Let's check.

Who: Riggan Thomas, a washed-up actor who played Birdman 20 years earlier.

Problem: Flailing career, broken relationships, in need of proving to the artistic community, and to himself, that he is relevant and talented. Adapting Raymond Carver's short story into a play that he is starring in and directing.

Goal: Get a successful review from Tabitha Dickenson, a top theater critic. This review will either make or break the play.

Stakes: His career, his belief in himself, his relationships, his life.

End: No one can say for sure. It's left up to interpretation. Does he jump out the window and die? Fly? The ending adds to the dark and surreal commentary on this man and his life.

So, as you can see, the idea is very lean. The goal is clear, and the stakes are high. We are following one man on one clear quest in which he will either reach success or not. Yet at the same time, the filmmakers have still infused surrealism, magic realism, darkly complex characters and highly surprising moments throughout the film.

Two Real Writers, Mary and Paul, Share Their Process to Find Solid Story Ideas

I often work with writers who think they know what they want to write about, when in fact, their ideas need to be honed a bit more before they are truly ready to write. Let's look at a few examples.

Example #1 — Mary's Story

Mary's idea: *I want to write about my abusive childhood.* (Mary is writing a memoir.)

Is this a story idea? No, not yet. It's an important kernel, but it needs to be fleshed out. I asked Mary to answer the Core Story Idea questions:

1. WHO is it about?

I want to write about myself as a teenager. I was shy, abused, frightened all the time and terrified of speaking out.

2. What **PROBLEM** did you encounter?

By 15, I had been abused by my stepfather and stepbrother for five years. Having kept the family secret all that time, when I saw that my younger sister was about to fall into the same fate at the hands of my stepfather, I took justice into my own hands and attempted to kill both men. This act landed me in juvenile hall, and I had to travel through the harsh and chaotic court system.

3. What was your **GOAL?**

My goal was to find justice for myself and later for other abused children and to learn how to speak in public when my "go-to" state of being was to hide and be mute.

4. What are the **STAKES?**

My freedom was at stake. Also at stake: my sense of self, my belief in the goodness of people and having hope for my life.

5. How does it **END?**

I was taken to trial and the truth of my childhood came out. By telling the truth and standing up for my sister and myself, I was able to find my courage and get into therapy to begin the healing process. The abusers were only slapped on the wrist, but with the truth out, my sister and I were allowed to move away from our abusive family members. We moved in with our aunt, and I began my lifelong crusade to help abused children speak out.

What Element Is Unique or Bold?

What people remember most about the story is that a peaceful, shy, 15-year-old Catholic girl turned to attempted murder.

Mary's Full Story Idea

Mary, a sexually abused, silent and scared 15-year-old girl, takes justice into her hands by nearly killing her father, fights her way through the harsh court system and becomes an advocate for abused children.

Example #2 — Paul's Story

Paul's idea: *I want to write about bioterrorism and how easy it would be to create a horrific crisis if one scientist goes rogue.*

Is this a story idea? Close. I asked Paul to answer the Core Story Idea questions:

1. WHO is it about?

At first, I saw it as a buddy film, following two patriotic, noble scientists who make a scary discovery in their lab. But then, I thought it might be stronger if we were primarily following Nick, a wealthy and lazy playboy who barely got his Ph.D., (and who we think has no real place in a lab). Nick is the youngest of four boys, and all of his siblings are accomplished and in high positions within the Washington system. Nick's father was abusive and demeaned Nick as a good-for-nothing since he could never keep up with his brothers. Instead Nick went the other way, embracing the life of the spoiled underachiever. Nick has never performed a courageous act in his life. And he never plans to.

2. What **PROBLEM** does Nick encounter?

Nick is a Washington D.C., playboy by night, and by day he works in a lab that is studying the effects of various strains of toxins. He got the job due to his father's connections and because the head of the lab, Dr. Crine, thinks he is too stupid and self-involved to realize what is actually going on. Nick comes to realize that Dr. Crine, though something of a lovable loser, is also unpredictable and mentally unbalanced. Nick does a little digging and uncovers that Dr. Crine is not who he is pretending to be. As Nick unravels the mystery behind the man, he finds out that his boss plans to sell a deadly strain of the toxin to an unknown and possibly more dangerous antagonist.

3. What is his GOAL?

Originally, I thought Nick's goal was to find his courage. Then I realized that was not specific enough and I transformed the goal to → Nick has to find his courage by stealing the deadly strain of the toxin before his boss can sell it.

4. What are the STAKES?

The lives of everyday citizens in Washington, D.C., Nick's belief in himself and his ability to be courageous.

5. How does it END?

Nick outwits Dr. Crine and is able to stop the terrorist attack. In doing so, he can face his biggest fear, that he is a man without courage. Unfortunately, no one else will ever know. Due to the top-secret nature of the threat, the government will not allow him to share how close the city came to a life-threatening bioterrorist attack. The story closes as Nick goes out at night to a club with all of his brothers and he is treated as he always has been, as a rich and flighty playboy. He's a changed man, yet no one knows but him.

What Element Is Unique or Bold?

This question helped me the most because, at first, it was coming out a little formulaic. But then I went back and did some research and some character work, and I made Nick a playboy and heir to a huge fortune, a man who could walk away from everything and live a fantastic life. He hates conflict, loves to get his way and has never had to have an ounce of courage to get anything in his young life. He is shocked to find out that he is actually quite smart, and even more shocked to find out that his life may have a purpose. I also worked on the antagonist, giving him a backstory that made the threat feel real and the man himself feel somewhat reasonable. In other words, you can almost understand why Dr. Crine is doing what he is doing once you know his history. What was unique in the end was that both the hero and the villain had relatable goals.

Paul's Full Story Idea

Nick, a playboy heir and low-level scientist, gets a job in a government lab purely out of nepotism. Underestimated by everyone, Nick uncovers the lab's horrific secret, that his boss is actually a dangerous bioterrorist bent on selling a deadly toxin to an enemy country. Nick must face his lack of courage, his less-than-stellar reputation and his mentally twisted boss in order to stop the diabolical plans to kill thousands of innocent people.

Note: It may take several attempts to come up with your story idea. Just try to be brief and make sure you include the five major elements.

EXAMPLES OF STORY IDEAS (You Already Know and Love)

The Wizard of Oz, by L. Frank Baum

Dorothy, a young girl who is running away from home, is whisked away by a tornado into a new world where she travels down the Yellow Brick Road to the magical and dangerous land of Oz, all in hopes of finding the Wizard and making her way home.

A Streetcar Named Desire, by Tennessee Williams

Blanche DuBois, a fading Southern Belle with delusions of grandeur and stories aplenty, moves in with her married (and newly pregnant) sister, Stella, in New Orleans. She is tormented by Stanley, her brutish, dominating and abusive brother-in-law, who makes it his mission to unravel her web of lies. As he confronts the disturbed woman, a painful, salacious truth is revealed, causing conflict that ultimately results in emotional and physical abuse that changes their lives forever.

One Flew Over the Cuckoo's Nest, **by Ken Kesey**

Upon being admitted to a mental institution, a rebellious and ornery patient rallies the other patients to take on the oppressive and harsh nurse who rules their lives.

Wild, **by Cheryl Strayed**

In the wake of her mother's death and her own divorce, Cheryl, sick and alone, makes the impulsive decision to take on the challenge of hiking more than 1,000 miles of the Pacific Coast Trail even though she has no experience or training. She takes this suspenseful and humorous trek alone, leading her on a journey that drives her crazy, gives her strength and ultimately heals her.

Tips for Making Your Story Idea Pop Off the Page:

- Utilize action words.
- Use descriptive words to add bits of color and flavor.
- Include your catalyst. Your catalyst is the call to action, the moment that will propel your protagonist into action.
- Describe your antagonist.
- Keep your story idea brief; the trick is to fill your story idea with all these elements but still keep it lean.

Soggy Story? Quick Fix

1. Make your protagonist want something a hell of a lot.
2. Make your antagonist want it more than the protagonist.
3. Make them opposites. Turn the conflict up. Make the stakes higher.

For example: In *A Streetcar Named Desire,* Blanche wants to live in her made-up world, and Stanley wants to break down all of her illusions. What's at stake? Blanche's sanity, Stella and Stanley's marriage, the fate of their baby, Stella's safety.

It could have been a story about a woman who moves in with her married sister.

The stakes are turned up by

- Making her sister an abused wife.
- Making Blanche an alcoholic, delusional woman with tales to tell and secrets to hide.
- Making Stanley a physically and emotionally abusive man who wants nothing more than to expose Blanche.

- Making Stella pregnant.
- Making Stella a woman who has never left Stanley, despite the ongoing abuse.
- Setting the play in a small urban apartment in New Orleans.

Q: When are you supposed to use the story idea tool?

A: I use **Who, Problem, Goal, Stakes and Ending** at all stages of the game. I use it when just starting out with a writer who is working on a brand new idea or with a struggling writer to diagnose what's not working. It can also easily transform a good story into an even better story. (Not to mention that it's a great tool to use if you ever need to pitch your story.)

Okay, so now we have a solid story idea.

Are we done?

Yes!

Extra Credit!

But no, not really. For those of you who like to do extra credit, I'm going to shepherd you along toward understanding why you are writing what you are writing.

The story idea is the *what*. The theme is the *why*.

A solid story idea is one that is happily married to the Umbrella Theme. (So, it's probably a good idea to know your theme so those two don't get a divorce.)

> **Q: What is an Umbrella Theme?**
>
> **A:** The unifying message of your story. It's truly what you, the writer, want to say to your audience. Themes are important because they travel throughout the story and act as a unifying force.
>
>
>
> Why do you want to tell this story?
> Why is it important for you? For others? What questions do you want your readers to ponder when they close the book or leave the theater?

Examples Of Umbrella Themes

The Wizard of Oz: You have the power inside you to grant your deepest wishes, if only you would believe in yourself.

Chekov's *The Seagull*: Humans have the odd (and maybe destructive) tendency to reject love that is freely given, yet seek it where it is withheld.

Romeo and Juliet: It's the battle of love and hate. Love has the overwhelming power to teach us how to step beyond our boundaries and limitations. If a society lets hate rule, everyone loses.

Q: So you can only have one theme in a story?

A: No. You can have several. But you want to try to pick an Umbrella Theme, the one that covers your most important message or question. You want to know what ideas you are exploring and what it is you are trying to say. And guess what? You want to know your theme even if your reader or audience does not.

Q: What if I don't know my theme yet?

A: Sometimes writers struggle with having to know why they are writing what they are writing. And it's true, you can absolutely write your piece first, then look back and reflect on its message. But to avoid some rewrite pain, try to think it through first.

Bottom line: Knowing your theme will help you craft a more cohesive story.

Knowing Your Umbrella Theme

Story Question → Reason for Ending → Message → Lesson

If you don't know your Umbrella Theme, you can uncover it by answering the following four questions.

(You already know your ending, having answered the Core Story Idea questions. Let's just take it a step further.)

The **questions** my story discusses are: _____
_____

A **reason for this ending** is: _____

A **message** you can take away from the story is: _____

A **lesson** my character learns is: _____

To walk you through an example of this process, let's continue with *Birdman*, which, arguably, may be one of the toughest cases out there when it comes to discussing theme. It's tough because the film's ending is left up to interpretation. In a way, the audience gets to determine their own message. (But this doesn't mean that the creators didn't know the unique message they wanted to impart.)

Ending: Riggan presumably jumps out the window to his death, yet his daughter looks out the window down at the street, then she looks up and smiles, as if she sees him flying.

In my estimation, the themes/ideas discussed in the film are

- Man's deep need to be relevant (to be seen and appreciated).
- Sometimes it's hard to tell the difference between fantasy and reality.
- The differences between high art and low art.
- Perception and truth.
- Resurrection.

***Birdman's* Umbrella Theme** (according to me—feel free to throw tomatoes): In this life, we blur fantasy and reality so that truth and perception are indistinguishable from one another.

Umbrella Theme Inspiration

You may have a lot to say and feel icky about trying to narrow it down. Don't fret! You can still say everything you want to say, but try to pick one Umbrella Theme for each book (or piece of writing) that you do. Your theme should be a statement or a question that expresses a universal message. If you're not sure where to begin, take some time to dance through the next few pages for some inspiration. Let's start with ideas that discuss universal life issues. Which ideas call to you the most?

Look for Your Theme in These Universal Life Issues:

1. Good and Evil
2. Birth and Death
3. Immortality
4. Finding Love or Losing Love
5. Lies and Betrayal
6. Ethics
7. Tragedy
8. Journey, Discovery or Conquering the Unknown
9. War, Peace and Patriotism
10. Technology/Humanity vs. Artificial Intelligence
11. Power, Manipulation or Corruption
12. Beauty, Aging and Vanity
13. Heroism, Glory
14. Money, Fame, Greed, Materialism
15. Facing Your Flaws
16. Working Class Struggles/Poverty
17. Escape from Internal or External Prisons
18. Sense of Self/Identity Crisis
19. Coming of Age

20. Hope and Hopelessness
21. Generation Gap, Aging
22. Home/Security of a Homestead
23. Loneliness or Isolation
24. Family: Blessing or Curse?
25. Rebellion: Individual vs. Society
26. God, Spirituality
27. Race Relations, Learned Racism
28. Suffering and Loss
29. Authentic Joy
30. Terrorism, Brutality
31. Courage, Duty
32. Power of Sexuality
33. Optimism and Pessimism
34. Temptation, Vice and Seduction
35. Ignorance vs. Knowledge
36. Conformity vs. Individualism
37. Power of Words and Writing
38. Deception and Appearances
39. Change vs. Tradition
40. Destruction of Innocence or Beauty
41. Dreams or False Dreams
42. Wisdom of Experience
43. Chaos vs. Order
44. Sacrifice of Self, Self-Preservation, Self-Control
45. Self-Reliance
46. Fate or Free Will?
47. Power of Nature, Man Against Nature, Beauty of Nature
48. Inner Strength vs. Outer Strength
49. Motherhood, Fatherhood
50. Oppression, Injustice
51. Overcoming Fear, Vice, Pain, Weakness
52. Pride, Silence
53. Traditional vs. Changing Roles (Men, Women)
54. Religion, Spirituality: Honorable or Hypocrisy?
55. Will to Survive

Theme Stew

A fun exercise I often do in workshops is to have people combine theme ideas to see what new and inventive ideas may surface.

Instructions: Pick two items from the list above and mash them up into a new stew.

Examples of Theme Stew Generated from a Workshop

1. Motherhood, God and Spirituality
2. Racism, Chaos and Order
3. Rebellion and the Will to Survive
4. Coming of Age and Deception
5. Change vs. Tradition During a Time of War
6. Good vs. Evil: the Destruction of Innocence
7. Power of Sexuality and the Brutality of War
8. Betrayal, Silence and Marriage
9. Power of Words, Silence and Aging
10. Inner Strength vs. Vanity
11. Intolerance, Poverty and Prisons

Readymade Themes → Pick a Theme, Any Theme

1. Love is stronger than death.
2. If you live by the sword, you die by the sword.
3. The meaning in life can be found in the circle of life.
4. You have to believe in yourself to achieve anything real.
5. Jealousy is a destructive force.
6. When men band together, they can defeat anything.
7. Absolute power corrupts absolutely.
8. You have to let go of the shore to reach new land.
9. Crime doesn't pay.
10. War is hell.
11. Technology is robbing people of their humanity.
12. You have more courage than you know.
13. Believe in your individual voice.
14. Don't let the light go out in your eyes.
15. One brave step leads to many.
16. There is life after loss.
17. You have to be your own hero.
18. Sometimes you have to escape the life you have to realize it really was the life you wanted.
19. Death is a mystery.
20. With death, there is an opportunity to be reborn.
21. There is an opportunity in every crisis.
22. Most journeys lead back home.
23. There is a moment in everyone's life when they come of age.
24. Being a patriot means you can question your leaders.
25. Hope springs eternal.
26. You never know anyone—not really.
27. Lust for power will leave you lost.
28. Everyone leaves this earth alone.
29. Justice is not blind.
30. Having it all isn't all it's cracked up to be.
31. Family is more important than anything.

32. Having faith is a leap.
33. Every man struggles with the good and evil within.
34. Families in today's world are disintegrating.
35. Man is small against Mother Nature.
36. Secrets never remain secrets.
37. Total conformity goes against a human's need to express him/herself.
38. Learned racism is toxic.
39. Suffering is part of the human experience.
40. We all lose our innocence.
41. You are never too old to reach for your dreams.
42. The present moment is all we have.
43. What comes around goes around.
44. Violence begets more violence.
45. There is no fate, only free will.

If you don't see it on the list, make up your own.

Okay, so now you have your story idea and your umbrella theme and you may be wondering: AM I DONE YET?

Oh, so close. One last question.

Does Your Idea Marry Nicely with Your Theme?

It's a damn good question and worth exploring. Let's look at one example to show you how I might walk a student through this last bit of the process. Let's go back to Mary's memoir. Remember her story idea: Mary, a sexually abused, silent and scared 15-year-old girl, takes justice into her hands by nearly killing her father, fights her way through the harsh court system and becomes an advocate for abused children.

How Mary Answered the **Theme Questions**:

- **Questions** my story asks →
Since I've been intimidated into silence my whole life, will I find my voice and stand up to my abusers? Will my life end before it begins? Can the cycle of abuse be stopped? How much courage do I have?

    Mary's Ending → *I discovered that my passion in life was to become an advocate for abused children and to help others.*

- **Reason for this ending** →
I think it's important to show how life's wounds can contribute to your life's purpose.

- Possible **message** →
No matter what you have been through, ultimately there is freedom in telling the truth and facing your demons.

- **Lesson** character learns →
I had more courage than I knew I had. By having the courage to speak my truth, I found out what I wanted to do was to help others to have courage.

So what is the theme or message of her story?

Mary's theme: Having the courage to speak your truth can provide courage for a lifetime.

Note: Mary chose the theme as the lesson she (as her main character) learned. Could there have been other themes? Yes, Mary toyed with a few others, some having to do with the injustice of abused children, some having to do with the cruelty of abusive parents. She decided that the above theme was the most unifying. In other words, it was her overall (Umbrella) message.

Does this theme fit nicely with her idea? Let's check:

Idea: Mary, a sexually abused, silent and scared 15-year-old girl, takes justice into her hands by nearly killing her father, fights her way through the harsh court system and becomes an advocate for abused children.

+

Theme: Having the courage to speak your truth can provide courage for a lifetime.

=

Mary, a sexually abused, silent and scared 15-year-old girl, takes justice into her hands by nearly killing her father, fights her way through the harsh court system and becomes an advocate for abused children. She comes to understand that having the courage to speak your truth can provide courage for a lifetime.

(Yay!)

Note: It may take several tries to come up with a concise theme; just stick with it, and you will get there.

Okay, time to try it out on your story.

Solid Story Idea Worksheet

Solid Idea

- WHO _____
  _____

- PROBLEM _____
  _____

- GOAL _____
  _____

- STAKES _____
  _____

- ENDING _____
  _____

Of these five elements, which one is particularly BOLD or UNIQUE?
_____
_____

Umbrella Theme

1. **Questions** my story explores are: _____
   _____

2. A **reason for this ending** is: _____
   _____

3. A **message** you can take away from the story is: _____
   _____

4. A **lesson** my character learns is: _____
   _____

Do my story idea and theme marry nicely? _____

Takeaway Lessons for Tool #2 Creating a Solid STORY IDEA

1. When you really know your story idea, and you can articulate your theme, you are damn near a rock star.

2. Solid vs. Soggy. A solid story idea can be expressed in one to three sentences. The reader can easily understand whom the story is about along with the central conflict that the protagonist is facing. A soggy story idea is one where the protagonist is not clearly defined, there is no clear-cut goal or forward-moving action, the theme is unclear, the stakes are low and the conflict is hard to understand.

3. There are many ways to describe the same idea—just get the major elements in there and keep it lean. It may take several tries to craft your story idea. Keep at it. You will get there.

4. To craft your story idea, answer five questions:

    WHO → PROBLEM → GOAL → STAKES → ENDING

5. Most writers struggle in the GOAL area. They resist giving their main character something SPECIFIC that he/she wants. Soggy story ideas often have characters who have no goal and/or low stakes.

6. The Umbrella Theme is the unifying idea, what you want to say to your audience (the message). To craft your theme, answer four questions:

QUESTION → REASON FOR ENDING → MESSAGE → LESSON

This is for the math geeks out there:

WHO → PROBLEM → GOAL → STAKES → ENDING

+

QUESTION → REASON FOR ENDING → MESSAGE → LESSON

=

SOLID STORY IDEA

TOOL #3

Dynamic CHARACTER Creation

Create Characters That Capture Your Audience's Imagination

"The story must be a conflict, and specifically, a conflict between the forces of good and evil within a single person." —Maxwell Anderson

What You Have Done So Far

Tool #1: By figuring out where you write best, how you write best and by creating a nurturing place to write, you have given yourself the best chance at writing success.

Tool #2: By working to craft a solid story idea and theme, you have laid a strong foundation upon which to build your story.

Now it's time to take that solid story idea and bring it all to life by adding in your compelling, kick-ass characters.

Q: What's the ultimate goal when writing characters?

A: Writing a character that pops off the page, that is constantly fascinating and that readers and audiences remember. Great thinkers and writers who have helped develop this character approach: Carl Jung, John Vorhaus, David Freeman, Linda Seger, John Truby, Linda Edelstein and Claude Levi-Strauss.

By the end of this chapter you will be able to

- Fill out the 9 Character Elements worksheet for each of your characters.
- Create a realistic character that is complex and rich—from the ground up.
- Understand your character's wants and motivations.
- Articulate what life-defining moment may be driving your character.
- Diagnose why a character may not be working. (And once you know the problem, you know how to fix it!)

Here's the damn truth about creating characters:

When I was working as a screenwriter, I found I would have one of two distinct experiences.

Characters either dropped into my lap fully formed and speaking to me from the get-go, or I couldn't get a handle on them and I struggled to find their voice. I see this experience repeated all the time with my clients. Sometimes a writer is able to download a fully formed character almost magically. This is where the writer seems to know everything about them intuitively (how they talk, walk, speak, dream). These characters dance from their fingertips as though they have always been there, just waiting to be written. Other characters, not so much.

This tool is for characters that

1. You want to develop from the ground up.
2. Feel fully formed but for some reason are coming out flat, lifeless or not fully developed.

Oh, I Got the Villain. Boy, Do I Have the Villain!

Sebastian, a writer in one of my read and critique groups, oh, so long ago, had a hard time with the idea that he was writing an incredibly boring hero. Week after week, the members of the group would tell him that his action hero was flat and a bit clichéd. To which Sebastian would always respond, "But what about the villain? Don't I have a great villain?" And he did. His villain came to him in a dream. He was original and bigger than life (he was a creepy, smart-ass Kentucky politician with a touch of sociopath).

Sebastian assumed that as long as *most* of his characters were formed, he was good to go, so he sent the manuscript out to agents. The feedback was, "Very interesting side characters, but found I was not invested in the main character." He came back to the group bummed out but finally ready to flesh out his main character. Yet, he had no idea where to start. He meditated. He did visual collages. He tried prompts and bought a ton of books on writing characters. He tried to force himself to have dreams about his main character, but nothing came. He tried the "write-to-find-it" method. This is where he just kept throwing his character into situations hoping that the voice might magically come alive. It didn't work. Nothing. Well, nothing to match his amazing villain. Sebastian came to me in total frustration.

I had had many experiences like the one with Sebastian. And I too was exhausted with the "Character Bible" method I was taught, wherein you needed to know everything about a character from the day he or she was born. Character Bibles made me impatient and just seemed unwieldy, and besides, they took way too damn long (remember: lazy writer, me).

I decided to look at all the elements that make up a character that feels completely "alive." I also looked at all of my therapeutic training and searched through hundreds of forms whereby real people did insight work to discover and uncover more about themselves. I wanted a tool that could speak to finding depth, quirkiness, likability and direction. And, I wanted something as fast and as painless as possible.

Thus, the 9 Elements of Character tool was born.

By walking Sebastian through these 9 Elements, he was able to swiftly locate the area that was not fully formed in his hero (the wound). He recrafted his hero and rewrote his manuscript, and the story took on wings. It was awesome to watch.

Q: How does it work?

A: If you have

1. **No character or a flat character** → use the tool to build from the ground up.
2. **A character that feels fully formed** → test it against the Character tool. See if you have missed "a biggie" or if you can learn something important about your character.

Following is the basic 9 Elements of Character worksheet beautifully blank:

9 Character Elements Worksheet

1. The BASICS:
Character Name: Age: Ethnicity:
Physical Shape: Financial Status: Location:
Religion/Political Affiliation: Occupation:

2. ROLE: (protagonist, antagonist, foil, surrounding major or minor)
_____

3. FLAWS: (selfish, rude, racist, angry, annoying, mean, lazy)
_____

4. LOVABILITY: (honest, kind, loyal, loves animals, smart)
_____

5. Character WANTS: (Character's overall goals/motivations/dreams. Don't censor yourself here. You will refine this into a specific plot goal/Outer Need soon.)
My character's **wants** _____

6. Character NEEDS: The *Outer Need* is what the character thinks he wants or needs; the *Inner Need* is what the character truly needs.

- **OUTER NEED:** Refine what your character wants into a SPECIFIC PLOT GOAL (solve the mystery, get the girl, get the promotion, get revenge, change body image, prove herself to the world) _____
- **INNER NEED:** What the character really needs (self-acceptance, to experience real love, to be awakened to life, to face the darkest demon, to risk, to find courage) _____

7. Character ARC: (Positive, Negative or No Change)_____

Positive Arc: (bad place to good place) _____
Negative Arc: (good to bad, neutral to bad or bad to worse) _____
No Change: (character makes no change during the story) _____

My character STARTS OUT: (scared, lost, doesn't believe in herself, hopeless, bitter)
_____

My character ENDS UP: (at peace, awake to life, with belief in himself, released of anger or bitterness, with hope) _____

8. WOUND: (Moment things changed, character was forever changed/hurt by life)
Life-Defining Wound:_____   _____

9. ARCHETYPE: _____

Frequently Asked Questions About the 9 Character Elements Worksheet

Q: Do I do a worksheet on EVERY character in my book?

A: Most writers do the worksheet on the top six to eight characters, but it certainly can't hurt to do it on any recurring character.

Q: Will every character have a dynamic character arc (one that changes)?

A: No. The character arc that is the most significant for your story is your protagonist's character arc. All other characters may or may not change. Generally, not everyone will change and grow by the end of the story.

Q: Can my characters have more than one archetype?

A: Sure, but try to stick to the top two—any more than that and your character can start to become fuzzy and unclear.

Q: How many Flaws/Lovabilities should my character have?

A: As many as you want. But in your story, I'd keep the focus on the top one or two. Narrowing it down creates a sharper, clearer character.

Q: How do I fill out the "Character Wants" section?

A: This is the place to pour out all your thoughts about what you think your character wants. You can babble or be as vague and/or rambling as you want to be. Example: "My character Delia wants to be happy. She wants to get married but she also wants to be a career woman. When Delia was 7, she dreamed she would be an astronaut and still somehow wants to do something monumentally significant."

Q: How do I fill out the "Inner and Outer Needs" section?

A: This is where you will want to get more specific.

- The Outer Need (or plot goal) is what the character thinks he needs to have, do, achieve or gain. Make it specific and clear. (Not just "to be happy" but to be happy by getting into Harvard and showing up her sister.)
- The Inner Need is what the character truly needs. Again, be specific in this section. (To love and accept herself no matter whether she gets into Harvard or not.)

Ready to walk through the 9 Elements? They are painless and quite informative, I promise.

Element 1: The Basics

The Basics are the baseline. Simply ground us with the knowledge of the character's name, age, ethnicity, physical shape, financial status, religion, political affiliation, location and occupation. No need to get fancy. Just the facts, ma'am.

Element 2: Character Role

It's important to know where your character fits in the story. Role tells you the character's job—the reason they exist in *this particular story*.

Characters' Roles/ Terms to Know

- **A Protagonist:** The main character (the story revolves around the protagonist).
  <u>The Protagonist's Purpose</u>: As the main character (and often the hero), the protagonist is the person we want to identify with, care about and most want to follow.
  <u>Writing Tips</u>: Keep the focus on the protagonist trying to achieve his or her goal. Many storytelling problems stem from this one issue. If you find that your story needs focus, meanders or wanders → take it back to the protagonist. So, when to use your protagonist? Almost ALL the time!

- **An Antagonist:** The character who works *against* your main character, who represents evil forces and/or is the major obstacle. *Note*: antagonist does not equal villain.
  <u>The Antagonist's Purpose</u>: As the opposing force to your protagonist and his or her journey, the antagonist is usually the person we want to dislike, conquer or fight against.
  <u>Writing Tips</u>: Keep the antagonist strong and active. Use the antagonist when you want to induce fear/conflict in your main character or when you need an agent to push the main character to change. Keep the antagonist present and have them grow in strength → make them a growing threat.

- **A Foil:** A character who is the contrast to another character. Most often we see foils as contrasts to our main character. Can be a buddy, a sidekick, an enemy or an opposite. (Charlie Brown's foil is Snoopy; Don Quixote's foil is Sancho Panza.)

<u>The Foil's Purpose</u>: As the person who helps to reveal who the main character is by being the contrast of that character. For example, a strong, courageous protagonist may have a fearful best friend as a foil. Can be a friend or an enemy. A sidekick or a competitor.

Writing Tips: Use the foil when you need to reveal aspects of the main character. To illustrate a character's intelligence, you can use a foil that is brainless. To illustrate a character's lack of compassion, use a foil who could compete with Mother Theresa. Foils can also overlap with other roles.

Got it? Now let's move on to discuss the other characters that you will use in your story:

- **Surrounding Major Characters:** The characters who populate the story, y'know, the ones we see all the time.

<u>The Surrounding Major Character's Purpose</u>: To populate the world. We usually get to know them pretty well and see them often. They help the protagonist along their journey by assisting or opposing them.

Here are three common Surrounding Major Characters:

The Confidant is a character that often serves as a sounding board, a voice of reason, a place to rest and be safe, a source of history, a support and a keeper of secrets.

<u>The Confidant's Purpose</u>: Use the confidant when the protagonist needs support, a gentle push, a rest, a sounding board, a kick in the ass, encouragement.

Writing Tips: The confidant can be used when you need your story to move in a new direction or when new or old information (sometimes exposition) needs to be imparted. The confidant need not be smart or helpful. In fact, the confidant may even push the protagonist in the wrong direction. But most of the time, the confidant is the good old best friend.

The Mentor is a character that serves as the voice of wisdom, the source of important information or special knowledge, the sage, and the window into other worlds.

The Mentor's Purpose: Use the mentor when the protagonist needs guidance, direction, to have his imagination sparked, to believe in herself.

Writing Tips: The mentor is used when the protagonist needs to move in a specific direction. The mentor will listen and act as a guide. The mentor is often used right around a plot movement or act break.

Note: The confidant and mentor may look similar. The major difference is that the confidant often listens and keeps secrets while the mentor acts as a guide. You can use both or just choose the one that works best for your story. There are no hard and fast rules here. Feel free to make these types work for your story.

The Love Interest is just that. The person the main character falls in love with. The love interest can serve as a confidant or mentor or just be the love interest (the one the protagonist makes goo-goo eyes at).

The Love Interest's Purpose: Use the love interest when the protagonist needs a goal or needs to be introduced to the warm and fuzzy aspects of life. Can also be utilized for the subplot and/or comic relief.

Writing Tips: The love interest can take the protagonist down a positive path or a negative path depending on the protagonist's arc. The love interest is often the opposite or complement to the protagonist (yes, they often complete one another).

- **Surrounding Minor Characters**: The characters that occasionally enter the plot for a specific purpose. Surrounding Minor Characters also serve to populate the world. They usually serve a very specific purpose (like a cop, hotel clerk or ticket agent). We may see them once or only on a few occasions. You need not do the worksheet on these guys (unless you really want to).

Examples of Character Roles in Stories You Probably Know

(Notice how some characters appear in more than one category.)

Cinderella (Disney's 1950 film)
Protagonist: Cinderella
Antagonists: Wicked Stepmother and Stepsisters
Foils: Stepsisters
Surrounding Major Characters: The Prince, The Fairy Godmother
Surrounding Minor Characters: The Animals—especially Gus and Jaq (the Mice), and Lucifer (the Cat)

The Wizard of Oz (L. Frank Baum):
Protagonist: Dorothy
Antagonist: Wicked Witch
Foils: The Scarecrow, The Tin Man and The Cowardly Lion
Surrounding Major Characters: Toto, The Scarecrow, The Tin Man, The Cowardly Lion
Surrounding Minor Characters: The Munchkins, People of Oz

Star Wars: (The 1977 movie—I'm old school—written and directed by George Lucas)
Protagonist: Luke
Antagonist: Darth Vader
Foils: Han Solo, Princess Leia
Mentor: Obi-Wan Kenobi
Surrounding Major Characters: Chewbacca, R2-D2, C-3PO, Grand Moff Tarkin (Vader's Boss)
Surrounding Minor Characters: Storm Troopers, Luke's Aunt and Uncle, Rebel Alliance Fighters

The Darker Side of Heroes, The Lighter Side of Villains

Though darker heroes and lighter villains have been around a long time, they are making a big comeback, especially on TV and in novels. Today's reader has come to expect characters that are more complicated and nuanced. So what does that mean exactly? It means that heroes are reflecting shades of villains and villains are reflecting shades of heroes.

If you think about it too much your head might start to spin sideways. I will try to make it less complicated. But first, I need a big disclaimer here.

Big Ole Disclaimer: This is one way to view what is going on with heroes and villains. I'm sure there are others. In my opinion, there's no one clean way to view this because so much of the time these definitions can overlap. For example, it's perfectly acceptable to say that there are instances when a character can be both an Anti-Hero and a Villain-Protagonist. My goal is to encourage you to see the complexity that we are now giving our heroes and villains so that you can compete in today's marketplace.

Let's start out by discussing some language and making it uber simple:

Hero: Good guy

Villain: Bad guy

Protagonist: Person whose goal we are following. (We usually want him to succeed.)

Antagonist: Person trying to block the protagonist from reaching their goal. (We usually want him to fail.)

(So the protagonist need not be a Hero, the antagonist need not be a Villain)

Good so far?

We are used to seeing the Hero as protagonist (good guy or gal seeking to do good). Examples: Superman, John Wayne, Jason Bourne in the *Bourne Trilogy*, John McClane from *Die Hard* and Katniss Everdeen of *The Hunger Games*.

We are also used to seeing the Villain as antagonist (bad guy or gal seeking to do evil). The bad guy who opposes the protagonist. Examples: The Wicked Witch in the traditional *Wizard of Oz* or Claudius in *Hamlet*.

But what if we want to incorporate shades of darkness in a traditional Hero or shades of lightness in a traditional Villain? New categories are born, such as Hero-Antagonist, Anti-Hero, Anti-Villain and Villain-Protagonist.

If you are trying to figure out what kind of character you should write, look to their motivation and the audience's amount of empathy for them.

7 ESSENTIAL WRITING TOOLS

Here's the chart that makes the most sense to me:

	Good	Morally Ambiguous	Bad
Protagonist (Story follows this character's goal, often story is from their Point of View)	Hero	Anti-Hero	Villain-Protagonist
Antagonist (Directly opposes the protagonist's goal)	Hero-Antagonist	Anti-Villain	Villain

When to use the Hero: When you want a clean, clear, traditional protagonist with recognizable heroic qualities.

Examples: Dorothy (*Wizard of Oz*), Clark Kent (*Superman*), Rocky Balboa (*Rocky*), Indiana Jones (*Raiders of the Lost Ark*).

When to use the Hero-Antagonist: When your protagonist is up to no good and someone has to stop them, or when you want us to have empathy for both the protagonist and antagonist.

Examples: Marshal Samuel Gerard (*The Fugitive*), U.S. Military (*The Hulk*), Carl Hanratty (*Catch Me If You Can*).

When to use the Anti-Hero: When you don't want a super squeaky-clean protagonist, when you want to make your protagonist more complex or dark.

Examples: Hamlet (*Hamlet*), Tony Soprano (*The Sopranos*), Jack Sparrow (*Pirates of the Caribbean*), Frank Abagnale Jr. (*Catch Me If You Can*).

When to use the Anti-Villain: When you want to lighten up or humanize the Villain. They tend to have some sympathetic qualities and sometimes have positive motivations, but mostly are just less evil Villains.

Examples: Magneto (*X-Men*), Frankenstein's Monster (*Frankenstein*), Godzilla, Metro Man (*Megamind*).

When to use the Villain-Protagonist: When you want an even darker protagonist. When you want to explore the idea of following a character with harmful goals and dark motivations.

Examples: Judah (*Crimes and Misdemeanors*), Travis Bickle (*Taxi Driver*), The Grinch (*The Grinch*), Clyde Barrow and Bonnie Parker (*Bonnie and Clyde*).

When to use the Villain: When you want to explore the darkest side of humanity, when your villain has few to no redeeming qualities.

Examples: Wicked Witch (*Wizard of Oz*), Martians (*War of the Worlds*), Cruella De Vil (*101 Dalmatians*), Claudius (*Hamlet*).

Story Examples

> ***Breaking Bad*** (AMC TV series, 2008–2013)
> Anti-Hero: Walter White
> Hero-Antagonist: Hank Schrader (DEA agent, brother-in-law)
> Anti-Villain: Gustavo Fring (Drug Kingpin)
> Villains: Tuco, The Cousins
> Foils: Jesse Pinkman (also a Confidant), Skylar White (Wife) and Walter White Jr. (Son)
> Mentor: Saul Goodman (Lawyer)
> Surrounding Major: Marie Schrader (Sister-in-law)

7 ESSENTIAL WRITING TOOLS

Surrounding Minor: Badger, Skinny Pete, Gretchen and Elliot Schwartz, Jane Margolis and Ted Beneke, Hector "Tio" Salamanca, Gale Boetticher

Hamlet (Shakespeare)
Anti-Hero: Hamlet
Hero-Antagonist: Claudius
Foils: Laertes, Fortinbras
Confidant: Horatio
Surrounding Major: Ghost of Hamlet's Father, Gertrude, Ophelia, Polonius
Surrounding Minor: Bernardo, Francisco, Marcellus, Rosencrantz, Guildenstern, Osric, The Players, The Gravediggers

The Player (1992 movie directed by Robert Altman, screenplay by Michael Tolkin)
Villain-Protagonist: Griffin Mill
Hero-Antagonists: Detectives Avery and DeLongpre (Suspect Mill is guilty of murder.)
Love Interest: Kahane's girlfriend, June Gudmundsdottir
Surrounding Major: Story executive, Larry Levy; writer, David Kahane; Bonnie Sherow (Mill's current girlfriend)
Surrounding Minor: Studio Chief of Security, Walter Stuckel; Tom Oakley and Andy Civella; Studio Head, Joel Levison; Mill's attorney

Want to know the best question ever when it comes to creating characters?

What Does the Story Need?

Not sure what character belongs in which role? Not sure if a character should be good or bad? Not sure if your protagonist should have a foil? Not sure how dark to make your hero?

"What does the story need?" is a question that I use all the time. (It's a super-duper and handy multipurpose question.)

Let's try it. Does the story need a really strong antagonist? Does the story need an antagonist who was posing as a confidant? (In that case they would be the antagonist, by the way.) Does the story need a foil for the main character to reveal an important characteristic of your protagonist? Does the story need a mentor that pushes the protagonist along the path?

Bottom line: Trust your story. It will tell you who belongs where and why.

Questions?

Q: What is an ensemble piece?

A: When there is more than one main character pushing the plot forward, you may have an ensemble piece, in which case the group itself is the main character. (Though often, one character stands out just a smidge above the others.)

Put a Face on It

Q: Can I make my antagonist an idea rather than a person?

A: In my humble opinion: no. While you may be inclined to think of an idea/concept/issue as the antagonist—like society, government, religion, etc.—you will want to create a character that represents the aspects of the idea you want to discuss. In other words, put a face on the concept. If you are writing about corrupt government, create a corrupt government official. If you are writing about a stifling religion, create an oppressive religious leader. Putting a face on the antagonist allows for more direct/specific conflict with your protagonist. (More conflict = more delicious story moments.)

Good so far? Let's move on.

Element #3: Flaws

Flaws are the juice. We humans are so wacky and weird and oh-so-deeply flawed. Flaws are what make us interesting. Flaws are what fuel the conflict. So don't shy away from flaws. I know it seems obvious that all characters should have flaws, but you'd be surprised how many characters are written without this important juicy goodness.

A good flaw can

- Be really fun to write about
- Spice up the conflict between characters
- Prevent the protagonist from getting what he or she most wants

Writing Tips: **For the protagonist, her major flaw is what she struggles to overcome.** Facing the flaw often happens at the climax and is due to the protagonist's new determination and/or skills. **For the antagonist, the major flaw is usually what brings him down and causes his downfall.**

Examples of juicy good flaws: sloppy, rude, sexist, racist, smelly, corrupt, lecherous, mean-spirited, lazy, stubborn, greedy, angry, insecure, addicted to substances, phony, prudish, weak, phobic, mentally unbalanced, filled with hubris, arrogant, prideful, insecure, fearful, incompetent, dim-witted, controlling, naïve, lacking self-esteem, obsessed, cynical, etc.

Element #4: Lovability "You just gotta love 'em."

Look, we readers will follow a character we love just about anywhere, doing just about anything. So give your character something that someone on the planet would find endearing. (Don't neglect your antagonist here.)

Bottom line: If we love 'em, we are hooked, and we are turning the pages.

Examples of lovability: loyal, honest, vulnerable, generous, kind, smart, strong-willed, funny, altruistic, light-hearted, dedicated, curious, innocent, gifted, filled with joy, adaptable, giving, authentic, pure, hardworking, stable, optimistic, self-aware, forgiving, charming, brilliant, hopeful, shy, noble, determined, open, tenacious, nerdy, talented, innocent, purposeful, etc.

Q: Can an adjective be placed in both the Flaw and Lovability section?

A: Yes. For example, "curious" could be both a flaw and a lovability factor. Not to be clichéd, but my cat is quite curious. This makes her lovable when she chases Luigi (the crazy-mean neighborhood cat) away from our backyard. It also makes her flawed when she chases Luigi up a 50-foot palm tree that she can't get down from for 10 and a half hours (despite all the super nice neighbors and their ladders, flashlights and enticing cans of tuna). By the way, it's totally false that the fire department will come get your cat out of a tree. Just sayin'.

Yo Mama So...

Otherwise Known As the "POP-UP PRINCIPLE."

Taken from the sophisticated principles used in a "Yo Mama" joke, this quick and dirty tool allows you to SEE the flaws or lovability of your character instantly.

How to Do It

Choose a word that describes the character's flaws or lovability. Place that word after "so," then complete the sentence below.

This character is so _____ that_____.

Example #1: Andrea was working with the flaw of *rule oriented*.

The character is so rule oriented that she would stop at a red light in the middle of the desert in the middle of the night and wait for it to turn green.

Example #2: Karen was working with the lovability of *dedicated*.

The little boy was so dedicated to his mission of saving the tiny baby raccoon that he set up a tent in his backyard for three nights in case the baby raccoon returned.

Okay, so far we've covered The Basics, Character Roles, Flaws and Lovability.

Let's look at a sample 9 Character Elements worksheet with the first half filled out so you can better visualize how it should look.

And yep, I'm going to use Dorothy from *The Wizard of Oz*. I use Dorothy 'cause I really like her, and chances are you're pretty familiar with her character and the story.

9 Character Elements Worksheet

1. The BASICS:
Character Name: *Dorothy Gale*   Age: *12 or 13*   Ethnicity: *White*
Physical Shape: *Healthy*   Financial Status: *Struggling*   Location: *Kansas*
Religion/Political Affiliation: *Unsure*   Occupation: *Student*

2. ROLE: *Protagonist*

3. FLAWS: *Impatient, doesn't appreciate what she has, doesn't believe in herself/in her own power to help herself.*

4. LOVABILITY: *Honest, pure, caring, loves her dog, Toto, cares for others she meets along the road, believes in others, courageous, fights for what she believes in.*

~~~~~~

Now moving on to...

Element #5: Character Wants

When analyzing a character that doesn't work, the problem is often basic. The character doesn't really truly want anything. This dynamic, unfortunately, creates a reactive character—or worse—an inactive character. Wants are movement. A character needs to want something so he or she can move forward.

Bottom line: Movement is interesting.

"In nearly all good fiction, the basic—all but inescapable—plot form is this: A central character wants something, goes after it despite opposition (perhaps including his own doubts), and so arrives at a win, lose, or draw."
—John Gardner

Let's go back to the premise at the beginning of Tool #3.

Q: What's the ultimate goal when writing characters?

A: Writing a character that pops off the page, that is constantly fascinating and that readers and audiences remember.

Make your protagonist want something, and don't let him get it (or not get it) till the VERY end. A character in motion, leading the charge, moving toward his goal goes a long way toward fascinating. Having said all that, a character's wants often grow and change as the story develops (and as the character sheds her Old Self/Old Ways). Characters often have three (or more) wants. They are defined as:

- → Original Want: What the protagonist/Old Self wants at the very beginning.
- → Developing Want: The want they will have for most of the story (most of ACT 2).
- → Ending Want: The New Self has new wants (often the want of ACT 3).

Did you know?

- Sometimes the Original Want is nothing, to be left alone or to <u>not</u> get involved.

- Sometimes the Original or Developing Wants are actually bad for the character.

- An Anti-Hero may be driven by good intentions, but their want is unhealthy, corrupt or evil.

"First, find out what your protagonist wants, then just follow him!" —Ray Bradbury

Let's look at some examples of Developing Wants:

Wizard of Oz
Original Want: to run away from home.
Developing Want: to find the Wizard of Oz so she can get home.
Ending Want: to believe in herself (and in her own ability to get herself home).

The Godfather
Original Want: to get as far away from the family business as possible.
Developing Want: to protect/be loyal to the family.
Ending Want: to run the family business.

Casablanca
Original Want: to be left alone, care for no one.
Developing Want: to be with Ilsa, help Ilsa, rediscover love?
Ending Want: to help Ilsa and her husband escape.

Breaking Bad
Original Want: to make enough money to help his family be secure after his death.
Developing Want: to make the best product, to be good at his job of making meth.
Ending Want: to rule a drug empire and get away with it.

Good to go? Then let's keep rolling.

Element #6: Outer Need and Inner Need
(Otherwise known as: It's not easy being human.)

Once you've identified what your character wants, this will serve as the Outer Need (often called a *plot goal*). But no character is complete without an emotional journey or an Inner Need. Let's look at this idea a little more closely.

Outer Need: What the character thinks he or she needs (plot goal).

Inner Need: What the character really needs (the lesson he or she needs to learn).

Q: Why must my character have TWO needs?

A: The answer to this goes back to a universal truth. That being: *What we want is not always what we need.*

We all walk around thinking we know what we need. Yet, ain't it true that sometimes we're wrong? (Come on: Think about that boyfriend or girlfriend or job that you simply had to have—yet in the end, it all went south.)

Now Hear This

Often a story appears to be about the Outer Need, but really it's about the Inner Need. In a story where a man sets off to make millions and is ignoring his family, his plot goal (Outer Need) may be to "make millions." Yet, his Inner Need may be to find the real worth in his life, quit his job and invest in his family.

Marni's purely anecdotal don't-quote-me-on-this-but-it's-totally-true observation

The reason I believe that well-drawn characters have an Inner Need and Outer Need is because they are reflecting our eternal human struggle.

We people think that outside accomplishments, people or material items will give our lives meaning or make us happy or fulfilled. (Outer Need)

Yet...

The only thing that truly helps us is to love ourselves no matter what. (Inner Need)

Let's look at some examples.

Breaking Bad – **Walter**
Outer Need: to make money, to be a successful drug dealer.
Inner Need: to save his soul, stop being a drug dealer.

***Wizard of Oz* – Dorothy**
Outer Need: to get to Oz in order to find the secret to getting home.
Inner Need: to believe in her own power.

***A Streetcar Named Desire* – Blanche**
Outer Need: hide from herself, believe her own lies.
Inner Need: believe in/accept herself for herself.

***Star Wars* – Luke**
Outer Need: defeat Darth Vader.
Inner Need: use the Force/believe in himself.

A Vorhaus Reminder: John Vorhaus reminds us that often in comic stories, no matter what the hero thinks he wants, what he really wants is love.

Important Note: The protagonist can have more than one Inner Need and Outer Need. But I will guide you to keep it to one major Inner Need and one major Outer Need to make your story stronger.

Did you know? Once you know your character's Inner Need, this information will assist you in finding the arc. Stay tuned. But first, more of that filled-out Dorothy character worksheet:

9 Character Elements Worksheet

1. The BASICS:
Character Name: *Dorothy Gale* Age: *12 or 13* Ethnicity: *White*
Physical Shape: *Healthy* Financial Status: *Struggling* Location: *Kansas*
Religion/Political Affiliation: *Unsure* Occupation: *Student*

2. ROLE: *Protagonist*

3. FLAWS: *Impatient, doesn't appreciate what she has, doesn't believe in herself/in her own power to help herself.*

4. LOVABILITY: *Honest, pure, caring, loves her dog, Toto, cares for others she meets along the road, believes in others, courageous, fights for what she believes in.*

5. Character **WANTS:** *To follow the Yellow Brick Road so she can seek help from the Wizard, to help her new friends along the way.*

6. This Character's **NEEDS:**

- **Outer Need:** *To get to the Wizard of Oz and go home.*
- **Inner Need:** *To go on a soul journey that helps her grow and appreciate home, to believe in herself.*

~~~~~~

We are on the home stretch now. Let's move on.

Element #7: Character Arc

Character arc: The change the character undergoes throughout the course of the story.

STATIC VS. DYNAMIC CHARACTERS

A DYNAMIC character changes and grows. He or she *moves through* a character arc. Dynamic characters are impacted by the plot. They learn, respond and grow in how they see/react to their world.

Q: What about my background characters that don't have a character arc?

A: These are the STATIC characters that essentially do not travel through a character arc and don't change. This type of character may start out depressed and lost and end up the same. Or remain happy and buoyant throughout the story—or grouchy or mean— you get the picture.

Do you know the role of a character arc?

- Serves as the character's route to internal change.
- Keeps the tension high and the conflict escalating.
- Often serves as part of the theme (the statement the author wants to make).

Four Types of Character Arcs: Positive, Negative, No-Change-Tragic and No-Change-Superhero. Let's look at each one of them for a brief moment.

> **Positive arc:** Character goes from a bad place to a good place in life = a Happy Ending.
>
> **Negative arc:** Character goes from good to bad, neutral to bad, or bad to worse = a Tragic Ending.
>
> **No-Change-Tragic:** The character remains the same throughout. Generally, protagonists who remain essentially the same

from beginning to end are fatally flawed. They have learned nothing from their experience and have shown no growth. This is tragic, as readers often want the protagonist to go through a journey and change = a Tragic Ending.

No-Change-Superhero: The character is already good and doesn't change (or maybe makes a slight change) = usually a Happy Ending.

Examples: *James Bond, Superman* and *Braveheart*. In these stories, the hero helps to change the world around him/her.

Note: If you want to have a protagonist that makes no change, make the character truly unique and unforgettable.

How to use the following table: Well, if you're writing a comedy or a story with a happy ending, then choose an element from "bad place" to start your character's arc and the corresponding element from "good place" to end the arc. If you're writing a tragedy or a story with a sad or bittersweet ending, then do the opposite.

Character Arc Table

BAD PLACE	GOOD PLACE
Weak	Strong
Lost/Not living	With new direction/Awake to life
Doesn't believe in herself	Believes in herself
Bitter	Released from bitterness
Angry	Released from anger
Hopeless	Hopeful
Alone	Connected to person or community
Lack of courage	Having found courage
Self-sabotaging	Aware and self-caring
Lack of ethics	Having found an ethical core
Stuck in failure	With new tools to succeed
Filled with guilt	Released from guilt
Self-loathing	Having found self-acceptance/love
Inability to love	Learning to love
In turmoil	At peace
Full of pride	Understanding humility
Stuck in the past	Ready to release past/move on
Stuck in the future	Moved on from failure/Ready to try once more
Holding on	Having let go
Controlling	Surrender/Acceptance

Are you unsure what your characters arc should be? Well, once you know the inner need it's actually quite easy to FIND THE ARC!

Why?

Because The INNER NEED = The Movement of the Arc

To Find the Arc in Three Easy Steps

1. Locate the Inner Need.
2. Decide if it's a Positive or Negative arc.
3. Locate where the character ends up and fill in the "STARTS OUT/ENDS UP" section of the worksheet.

To walk you through this, let's go back to authors Mary and Paul, our examples from the previous chapter.

Example #1 – Mary's Story

Remember: Mary's Full Story Idea

Mary, a sexually abused, silent and scared 15-year-old girl, takes justice into her hands by nearly killing her father, fights her way through the harsh court system and becomes an advocate for abused children.

1. Locate the Inner Need

Mary: to find the inner courage and speak out.

2. Decide on a Positive or Negative arc to determine where the character ends up.

Reminder → Positive arc: Where she ends up is the opposite of where she starts out, achieves arc, better off.

Reminder → *Negative arc: Unable to achieve arc and/or worse off than where she started.*

Positive arc → Mary finds a way to uncover her courage and use her voice.
Negative arc → Mary is never able to uncover her courage and use her voice.

Mary's story was a Positive arc → Mary finds a way to uncover her courage and use her voice.

3. Locate where the character ends up and fill in the "STARTS OUT/ENDS UP" section.

STARTS OUT: scared and silent.
ENDS UP: courageous and speaking up.

Example #2 – Paul's Story

Remember: Paul's Full Story Idea

Nick, a playboy heir and low-level scientist, gets a job in a government lab purely out of nepotism. Underestimated by everyone, Nick uncovers the lab's horrific secret, that his boss is actually a dangerous bioterrorist bent on selling a deadly toxin to an enemy country. Nick must face his lack of courage, his less-than-stellar reputation and his mentally twisted boss in order to stop the diabolical plans to kill thousands of innocent people.

1. Locate the Inner Need

Paul: to release his narcissistic and selfish approach to life.

2. Decide on a Positive or Negative arc to determine where the character ends up.

Positive arc → Nick finds a way to release his selfish approach to life and fight for the lives of others.
Negative arc → Nick is unable to find a way to release his selfish approach to life and doesn't fight for the lives of others.

Paul chose a Positive arc (though he toyed with a Negative arc for months!). → Nick finds a way to release his selfish approach to life and fight for the lives of others.

3. Locate where the character ends up and fill in the "STARTS OUT/ENDS UP" section.

STARTS OUT: selfish, without purpose.
ENDS UP: selfless, with purpose.

Other Examples of Arcs

→ **Charlie Babbitt (Tom Cruise) in *Rain Man***

Beginning of arc: Babbitt is a ruthless car dealer who kidnaps his autistic brother because he feels cheated about not receiving any money from his father's will.
End of arc: After a cross-country journey with his brother, he learns the importance of family and turns down the money.

→ **Cheryl Strayed (Reese Witherspoon) in *Wild***

Beginning of arc: Is lost, reeling from trauma, in need of healing.
End of arc: Having gone through a spiritual journey, experienced some healing.

→ **Michael Corleone (Al Pacino) in *The Godfather***

Beginning of arc: Wants nothing to do with his father's crime business.
End of arc: The head of his father's crime syndicate.

→ **Travis Bickle (Robert De Niro) in *Taxi Driver***

Beginning of arc: A slightly disturbed, chaotic Vietnam Vet.
Ending of arc: A highly organized, full-blown psychotic.

→ **Melvin Udall (Jack Nicholson) in *As Good as It Gets***

Beginning of arc: Is closed, rigid, not willing to change.
End of arc: Open, heart softened, willing to change.

And Now for a Wee Bit About *Bittersweet* and *Subtle* Endings

If you're reaching for a bittersweet or melancholy ending

- Have the character achieve some of the arc *but not all*, or some of what she wants and needs *but not all*.

If you want to make the character arc less dramatic or reach for a subtle ending

- Don't let your main character master the "good place." They're just open to learning, open to doing things differently and/or ready to try again.

Quiet Can Be POWERFUL

A character arc doesn't have to be huge or one where he or she saves the world. Often the quietest moments are the ones in which characters find their greatness. The moments that truly define us are almost always quiet and deeply personal. They are the moments that no one else may see, times when we're able to overcome our limitations and rise to be something more.

Tips to Crafting a Real, Believable Arc
(OR, THEY GOTTA FALL DOWN, A LOT)

So, exactly how does a character go from *a bad place* to *a good place* or vice versa?

<u>Soggy character arcs</u>: sudden, jumping movements or shifts; huge leaps in behavior.

<u>Solid character arcs</u>: natural, step-by-step movements that show the behaviors being challenged, confronted and changing slowly.

Real change requires convincing, believable development.

Have you ever tried to change a habit? Yeah, it sucks. It's really hard and, most often, it doesn't happen overnight. It often works with a "two steps forward, one step back" movement. Therefore, your character should travel along his or her arc, usually unwillingly, all the while wrestling with and eventually overcoming some or all of his or her flaws or limitations. A character will almost always return to their poor behavior several times before relinquishing it.

- The character travels.
- The character wrestles with what he finds on the road.
- The character fails, tries again, gets back on the road and travels, wrestles, fails, and tries again.

Simply stated: Events and people confront the character and his flaw until he is forced to face the truth about his flaw, and, in doing so, will make the *conscious choice* to change or not to change.

Now, here's an easy tool to use if...

Creating a "Natural-Feeling" Character Arc is Messing with Your Head

Q: I'm still struggling with creating an arc that feels natural. What do I do?

A: Try the Old Self to New Self—Progression Chart.

Every character starts out as their "Old Self." Some make it to a "New Self," some do not (or their New Self is even worse than their Old Self). If you're struggling to make your character's arc real and believable, fill out the:

> Old Self → New Self—Progression Chart
>
> 1. Old Self → Flaw
>
> 2. Struggling Self → Struggling with the flaw, flaw is winning
>
> 3. Emerging Self → The flaw loses sometimes; New Self is starting to shine
>
> 4. Last Big Decision → A decision is presented. The character can have what he always wanted, but he keeps doing business as usual, which means holding on to his flaw. If he chooses a new way, it's scary and out of his comfort zone. Making this decision means accepting his New Self, no matter how scary.
>
> 5. New Self → Flaw is either gone or greatly diminished

Ready to move on? Good, 'cause it's time to learn a bit about character depth.

Element #8: Finding the Wound

Everyone gets hurt by life. Sad fact, I know. But *how* you get hurt often defines your point of view about life and, ultimately, your actions.

Discovering a character's life-defining wound helps
- Develop sympathy or empathy for the character.
- Flesh out the character.
- Add depth to the character and story.

Discovering Your Character's Life-Defining Wound

Note: You may want to try this out on yourself first. I have all my students do it first on themselves, and somehow this brings the impact of the exercise home.

Instructions

1. Pick three not-so-great moments in your character's life that you think made a big impact on his or her life or affected them deeply. Look first to moments in childhood.

2. Of the three, which one stands out the most?

3. How has this moment made an impact on his or her life?

Examples from real writers' actual characters: **Sharon**, **Fitz** and **Danny**

Sharon — *Moments*
1. Day her brother was killed (age 7).
2. Day she found out that her husband was cheating (age 26).
3. Day she didn't get into college (age 17).
Chosen Moment: Day brother was killed (age 7).
Impact: She learned that things you love in life can be taken away, stopped believing in God, trusted much less.

Fitz — *Moments*
1. Day his father took away the car he had bought him (age 16).

2. Night he saw his father beat his mother up for the first time (age 6).
3. Day they lost their family business (age 12).
Chosen Moment: Day dad took away his car (age 16).
Impact: He went out and saved all summer for a new car. Experienced pride and a lesson about standing on his own two feet. Learned he can and should rely on himself.

Danny — *Moments*
1. Day his father died at war (age 4).
2. Day his mother tried to kill herself (age 9).
3. Day he realized he was an addict (age 23).
Chosen Moment: Day his mother tried to kill herself (age 9).
Impact: Learned that, at times, he is powerless when it comes to the ones he loves, that letting go was the only way he would survive.

Now we move from the arrow-in-the-heart to something a bit more fun. (And we're almost done!)

Element #9: Archetypes—The Grounding Force

The last of the 9 Elements is learning your character's archetype. Knowing the archetype will assist you in creating a character that has a distinctive voice.

"In using archetypes, the essence of your character is narrowed down so she jumps off the page at the reader instead of blending in with all the other characters." —Victoria Schmidt, author of *45 Master Characters*

Marni Works in an Office

I'm terrible in an office. Bad, bad, bad with office politics, really bad about turning paperwork in on time and terrible about sitting at my desk (turns out they really want you to sit there, like, a lot). The only way I survived was to know my archetypes. What are they? In my mind, it was knowing who would be doing what if the ship started to sink.

Here's how it worked. Sometimes, I would sit in a boring Tuesday morning team meeting and categorize each person. In other words, I would figure out their archetype. I would ask myself, *if the ship started to sink*:

- → Who would get practical and look for lifeboats and life vests?
- → Who would get on the lifeboat first without a care for others?
- → Who would freak out, panic and make things worse?
- → Who would want paperwork done about the ship sinking?
- → Who would help other people that were panicking?
- → Who would rush to the helm to see if he/she could help right the ship?
- → Who would scream, "It's all his fault!" and find someone to blame?
- → Who would pretend it wasn't happening?
- → Who would play the violin as the ship went down?
- → Who would get vodka and cranberry juice?

Maybe it was a horribly insensitive practice, but I swear it worked. Knowing the archetype would tell me who I could trust, who I couldn't, who to go to in a time of need and who to steer clear of *no matter what*.

Whenever I work with a writer who has a character that's not working, uncovering the archetype and playing with it has often solved the problem. I'm not saying it's a magic bullet, except I totally think it's a magic bullet.

Now wait, no understanding of archetypes is complete without a basic introduction to

Carl Jung. Jung was a Swiss psychiatrist (1875–1961) and influential writer/thinker whose lifework made a deep impact in both literature and psychology. He was a close collaborator with Sigmund Freud before he broke away, founding the field of analytic psychology. For our purposes here, and simply put, he analyzed behaviors and personality types and categorized them into archetypes. (If you're even slightly interested in Jung, look deeper. He makes you think, then think again, in all the best ways.)

Many writers shy away from using archetypes. They fear they will be writing a stock character—one that lacks originality, depth and complexity. Ironically, knowing the archetype can assist you in creating a character with depth and complexity. Also, you can make your archetype original by placing him/her in an unexpected role.

Still Not Convinced?

Q: But why, oh why, should *I* use archetypes?

A: Here are some good reasons:

- Makes a story feel fully developed. Knowing the archetypes can help your world feel complex and real.
- It contributes to identifiability. People will feel they know someone "just like that."
- Assists with writing believable group dynamics. If you want real group dynamics, take a handful of archetypes and throw them in a room together and let them duke it out.
- Conflict between archetypes creates tremendous dramatic tension.
- Archetypes perform essential functions that may be necessary for your story. You may need a character to point your protagonist in the right direction or the wrong direction. You may need a character to offer advice, provide wisdom or present specialized knowledge. You may need a character to push the protagonist into facing his fears. You may need a character to be the voice of temptation, faith, logic or purity. All these voices stem from archetypes.
- It's a grounding force. When we see/read an archetype though he may look a particular way, the audience is grounded in knowing who he is in some deep, unexplainable way.

John Truby, storytelling guru and author of *The Anatomy of a Story*, states: "*Using archetypes as a basis for your characters can give them the appearance of weight very quickly, because each type expresses a fundamental pattern that the audience recognizes, and this same pattern is reflected both within the character and through interaction in the larger society.*"

Q: How can I avoid writing stock types or stereotypes?

A: Stereotypes are different than archetypes. A stereotype is a generalization and often rears its head out of prejudice. An archetype comes not from superficial judgment but out of the collective consciousness, what we as human beings see in one another and have for many, many years on the planet.

Q: How do I work with the archetype to make it my own, original character?

A: Three answers.
1. Find the archetype you think is a good fit (or something you can play with). Use it as a grounding force, a launching point, as inspiration. Let your creativity take over from there.
2. Go against expectation. Place the archetype in an unexpected role. Examples: Put a child in the role of antagonist. Put a clown in the role of mentor. Put a trickster in the role of protagonist.
3. Combine two archetypes.

FYI: Another cool tool is the Enneagram. The Enneagram is a visual and spiritual tool for mapping personality and breaks personalities into nine categories. To learn more about it go to: www.enneagraminstitute.com

Following, you will find my big fat list of 55 Character Archetypes. Select the one that most represents your character, or ones that you want to play with. Experiment and see for yourself whether or not it gives your character more weight.

THE BIG 55 Character Archetypes From A-Z

Artist: Sensitive, withdrawn, expressive, dramatic, self-absorbed, temperamental, romantic, visionary, full of passion, creativity and intensity, spontaneous, loving, loves to impact change, trouble controlling emotions, takes things to extremes, unaware of boundaries.

Beast: Physically unattractive but with humanity, or physically attractive but without humanity, a representation of the primitive past of man.

Boss: The leader of the pack, the "go-to person," the solver of problems, may be overbearing and controlling, competitive, stubborn, aggressive, status-seeking, can be chronically rude.

Career Criminal: Commits crime with high stakes, smart, suspicious, may be highly skilled, plans carefully, may move often, can be charming, feels like an outcast, creates their own morality.

Child: Can be young in age or spirit, loves adventures, seeking play and playmates, potential, innocence, rebirth, salvation, believes in good vs. evil.

Clown/Joker: Uses humor to cope and avoid tough emotions/intimacy, serves as happy distraction, makes others happy by joking around/diffusing the tension, may be sad inwardly, does not show this to outsiders, thinks he is helping people by relieving stress. (*Note*: A more pure form of this archetype is **The Jester**, always lighthearted and joking but pure of heart and truly caring for others, like Kramer in *Seinfeld*.)

Doer/Achiever: Focus is on success, often has experienced success, frequently building a track record, great ability and ambition, at times cannot see the bigger picture and loses out on love/family/living in the moment due to single-mindedness. Organized, driven and often needs to be seen as a winner. Rarely stands still.

Emotionally Sick: Mentally unhealthy, dependent, sometimes the focal point of the family, can create chaos, draining on others.

Enabler: Maintains group balance by rescuing the irresponsible one and smoothing things over. Often faces a dilemma: If they do not bail the irresponsible one out of a bad/dangerous situation, the irresponsible one could do serious harm to self or others. May be contributing to the irresponsible behavior by continuing to rescue and cover up—but believes that they are simply being helpful.

Father: Source of authority and protection, powerful, strict, often induces fear, protects loved ones fiercely, wants to win, can be an activist, very physical, motivated by survival, can be career focused, sometimes fails to think things through.

Feminist: The female cause is her cause and fighting for equality for all. In extreme cases, the masculine side is just as strong as her feminine side, intuitive, instinctual, task-oriented, self-sufficient and goal-oriented.

Femme Fatale: Seductive, charming, loves being in control, loves the thrill of the chase, often provokes jealousy, has star quality, fashion conscious.

Flamboyant/Show Off: Extrovert who likes to be the center of attention, extreme need to display intelligence, talent or body, often deeply insecure, overcompensates for a deep need to be loved/find connection, can be dramatic and easily upset, flaky.

Fool: Still a little boy or girl inside, seeks to play/find a playmate, wanders off in confusion with faulty directions, creates chaos for others, cares for children, takes risks, avoids commitments and responsibility, fears boredom, loves freedom, can be charming.

Girly Girl: Innocent, feminine, focused on beauty and all things girly, can be extremely naïve, helpless or dependent, idealistic and coy, nurturing, passive, difficulty expressing anger or dealing with conflict, boosts men's egos, may doubt own adequacy, flirtatious.

God or Goddess: All powerful, source of magic, can provoke fear, awe, humility, the Great Mother or Mother Earth.

Guy's Guy: Masculine in an exaggerated way, rugged, tough, fearful of weakness, adventurous, aggressive, worldly, sexually experienced, ambitious, needs to win, risk taker, may have rocky relationships with women.

Imposter/Pretender: Takes advantage of situations, intelligent, verbal, delights in deceiving people, looks for weakness to exploit it, may make a career out of deception, makes his own rules, rationalizes his life choices.

Investigator/Thinker: Withdrawn, intense, cerebral, perceptive, innovative, secretive, isolated, can become obsessed/highly focused on a goal. Finding what is hidden/unknown brings creative joy.

Irresponsible: Avoids commitment, dedicated to the moment, to his freedom, fears being chained down to a schedule, can turn to drugs and alcohol, lives life on his terms, discounts societal rules, selfish, narcissistic, creates chaos by acting on desires, destabilizes the group.

Journeyman/Hero: Journeys on a quest, champion, defender, rescuer, travels on journey to realize his/her destiny, can lose sight of all but the journey, often reluctant to go on journey, to be a fully realized hero he must face his greatest fears and flaws.

King: Ruler, sees the big picture (often avoiding the details), cares for the whole village, can be authoritative, lacking emotion, can be an addict, craves self-esteem and self-respect, confident, strategist, needs a kingdom, can be controlling, fear provoking, stoic, unable to express emotions.

Know-It-All: Superior attitude, can be self-absorbed, tries to come across as having it all together but often just seems silly, full of it, low self-esteem, needs to be seen as an expert, may try to change others or the situation.

Loner: Isolated, struggles to connect with others/socially inept, avoids conflict, invested in his or her rich inner world only, fears the world, usually intelligent, reliable, loyal, trusts few, can have a large imagination, feels alien to others.

Lover/Love Interest: Romantic, sincere, dedicated to object of his or her affection, often poetic or artistic, often the symbol of home base or security, believes in the protagonist, the person the protagonist can vent to.

Loyalist: Strong ability to support others, bonds and stays, can lack self-worth, doubts abilities, tends to isolate when not with specific loved ones, bighearted, can get behind a cause.

Magician or Shaman: Offers an elixir, explains the mysteries of life, may provoke fear in others, spiritual, powerful, often loves to be alone/dislikes the spotlight.

Maiden: Innocent, full of desire, pure, often searches to be rescued, inexperienced and naïve, often self-confident, playful, takes risks, may want to party and have fun, can be sexy or child-like.

Manipulator: Charming, intelligent, ability to read the needs of others and use the information, sly, deceitful, crafty, may appear attractive at first or on the surface, ability to pull others in, can play the role of the backstabber.

Mentor: Advisor, expert, intelligent and wise, wants to be in protagonist's life, cares for protagonist, can be positive or negative force in protagonist's life, may be in a competitive relationship with protagonist, and mentor may be struggling to let go.

Mother: Source of nurturing and comfort, calming, center of the hearth, offers guidance, can be over-controlling and full of worry, sense of duty to help others is strong, can be needy, a martyr, passive-aggressive.

Narcissist: Self-absorbed, inability to see the needs of others, draws the attention back to himself, often a show-off, low self-esteem, lacks empathy for others, needs to be admired, will express his grandiose sense of self, often a politician or religious leader due to ready, admiring audience.

Nemesis/Challenger: A friendly troublemaker, has a surface-friendly relationship with the protagonist, but his or her main goal is to mess up the protagonist's life, often jealous, the nemesis loves to hate the protagonist—in fact, it's part of their life's purpose.

Observer: Watches all but often quiet. Usually a deep thinker and when he or she does speak, it's something of importance, insight or gravity. Will withhold judgment until all the evidence is in. Can be fiercely loyal to the protagonist or his tribe. Has trouble letting loose and having fun.

Peacemaker: Tries to be the force of peace, dislikes conflict, easygoing, self-effacing, receptive, reassuring, agreeable, complacent.

Perfectionist/Conformist: Needs precision, pressures others to reach for the best, hard on themselves/others, can be rigid, purposeful, finds it painful to live outside society's expectations, cares deeply what others think, anxious, can be a team player, finds meaning and stability in rules and regulations.

Pessimist/Depressive: Glass half-empty point of view, pulls others down, self-absorbed, "Debbie Downer," will offer disapproval, "why try?" attitude, will take no risks, spreads doubt, defeat, confusion. Ruled by depression.

Psychopath: No conscience, amoral, inability to feel or care for others, no sense of guilt or consequences, can be a source of fear, easily bored, motivated by money, impulsive, irresponsible, no sense of belonging, no strong emotions, rationalizes their behavior.

Queen: Ruler, willing to sacrifice herself for the greater good, can be stoic, has masculine qualities, can be the bringer of harsh truth, stands up for beliefs, protective, loyal, wants to keep order, strong, can be boastful.

Rage-Filled: Goes from irritated to fury quickly, violent, can't control temper, dislikes most people, often self-loathing, loyal. Ironically, when calm can be loving, likes to laugh and be passionate.

The Reformer: Rational, idealistic, principled, purposeful, self-controlled, often a perfectionist.

The Robot/Intellectual: Hides in their knowledge, intelligence trumps feelings, may struggle socially, low-communication skills, high abilities, strength can lie in their objectivity. The "techie" version of this archetype hides in technology, has little contact with people and the outside world.

Scapegoat: The one to blame when things go wrong, the person who acts out in a dysfunctional family, often the one who receives all the negative attention. (The acting-out teen sent to therapy who deals with drunken father nightly but is seen as the "sick one.") Can be rebellious, perhaps antisocial, "juvenile delinquent."

Scaredy-Cat/Fearful: Worrier, anxious, brings fear/panic to others, hides from life and new experiences, the member of the group who will bring up what might go wrong in any scenario. Ruled by anxiety.

Trickster: Troublemaker, liar, rascal agent that pushes us toward change, self-absorbed, can be entertaining or charming.

Troubled Teen: Hates rules, defies authority, can be depressed, self-centered and angry, loyal to fellow criminals, feels above the law, vulnerable (cults and drugs).

Upside-Down Hero/Anti-Hero: Motivated by base or lower-nature drives, driven by pursuit of power, sex, money, control, need to fill his or her appetite, which is big and often all that matters. Can be selfish, anti-social, power-hungry, materialistic. (By examining the dark side of an Anti-Hero, the audience may be able to explore/come to terms with their shadow side.)

Warrior Hero: Takes action, takes on causes, fights for what he believes, single-minded, leads the pack, craves blood and battle, most in touch with rage/anger as primary emotions, takes risks to compensate for loneliness, doesn't expect to live long.

Wild One/Flamboyant/Rebel: Cares little what others think, walks to the beat of her own drum, often likes to shock/display her different/offbeat worldview, against the grain of society.

Wise Old Man/Woman: Sage, guide, keeper of profound knowledge, offers wisdom, has "seen it all."

Wizard/Psychic: Eccentric, possesses knowledge about hidden secrets of the Earth and the spirit world, often sought out when magic or transformation is needed. The Psychic may possess knowledge of other worlds or the future.

Woman's Man: Loves women above all else, women love him and are drawn to his inspirational, passionate qualities, smooth talker, motivated by love and belonging, yet may have trouble committing, searching for impossible ideal, can be irresponsible/flighty, sensual and erotic, can be seen as a dreamer, chivalrous, gentle, driven by experiences.

Vampire: Uses people for his or her needs. Passionate, sometimes romantic, experiences life in a heightened way, strong emotions, self-absorbed, can be dominating and secretive.

Victim: Often adopts a "poor me" mentality, believes he will always suffer, looks for evidence that life is working against him.

Zombie/Monster: Half human or not human at all, provokes fear, panic, sometimes has human qualities/elements. Sometimes the monster has more humanity than the humans that surround him/her.

Now, here is Dorothy Gale's completed Character Elements worksheet:

1. The BASICS:
Character Name: *Dorothy Gale*   Age: *12 or 13*   Ethnicity: *White*
Physical Shape: *Healthy*   Financial Status: *Struggling*   Location: *Kansas*
Religion/Political Affiliation: *Unsure*   Occupation: *Student*

2. ROLE: *Protagonist*

3. FLAWS: *Impatient, doesn't appreciate what she has, doesn't believe in herself/in her own power to help herself.*

4. LOVABILITY: *Honest, pure, caring, loves her dog, Toto, cares for others she meets along the road, believes in others, courageous, fights for what she believes in.*

5. Character **WANTS:** *To follow the Yellow Brick Road so she can seek help from the Wizard, to help her new friends along the way.*

6. This Character's **NEEDS:**

- **Outer Need:** *To get to the Wizard of Oz and go home.*
- **Inner Need:** *To go on a soul journey that helps her grow and appreciate home, to believe in herself.*

7. Character ARC: *Positive*

STARTS OUT: *Doesn't believe in herself/doesn't appreciate home.*
ENDS UP: *Believes in herself/appreciates home.*

8. WOUND: *Unsure, but she has been orphaned and is living with her aunt and uncle in a town where they are bullied by people with more money and influence. Her wound probably has to do with wondering if/where she belongs.*

9. ARCHETYPE: *Maiden/Journeywoman*

Extra Credit!

For more Character Tools and a World-Building worksheet, see Appendix 3. (The Defense Mechanism Tool is pretty cool.)

And here's another blank 9 Character Elements worksheet!

9 Character Elements Worksheet

1. The BASICS:
Character Name: Age: Ethnicity:
Physical Shape: Financial Status: Location:
Religion/Political Affiliation: Occupation:

2. ROLE: (protagonist, antagonist, foil, surrounding major or minor)
_____

3. FLAWS: (selfish, rude, racist, angry, annoying, mean, lazy)
_____

4. LOVABILITY: (honest, kind, loyal, loves animals, smart)
_____

5. Character WANTS: (Character's overall goals/motivations/dreams. Don't censor yourself here. You will refine this into a specific plot goal/Outer Need soon.)
My character's **wants** _____

6. Character NEEDS: The *Outer Need* is what the character thinks he wants or needs; the *Inner Need* is what the character truly needs.
- **OUTER NEED:** Refine what your character wants into a SPECIFIC PLOT GOAL (solve the mystery, get the girl, get the promotion, get revenge, change body image, prove herself to the world) _____
- **INNER NEED:** What the character really needs (self-acceptance, to experience real love, to be awakened to life, to face the darkest demon, to risk, to find courage) _____

7. Character ARC: (Positive, Negative or No Change) _____

Positive Arc: (bad place to good place) _____
Negative Arc: (good to bad, neutral to bad or bad to worse) _____
No Change: (character makes no change during the story) _____

My character STARTS OUT: (scared, lost, doesn't believe in herself, hopeless, bitter)
_____

My character ENDS UP: (at peace, awake to life, with belief in himself, released of anger or bitterness, with hope) _____

8. WOUND: (Moment things changed, character was forever changed/hurt by life)
Life-Defining Wound: _____ _____

9. ARCHETYPE: _____

Takeaway Lessons for Tool #3 Dynamic CHARACTER Creation

1. The major character roles include protagonist, antagonist, foil, love interest and mentor/confidant. You can have many minor characters that help fill out your world.

2. Flaws and Lovability are essential aspects of a character that help make him/her feel real. It helps us to be drawn both to and away from a character.

3. The number-one place writers falter with characters is not making them ACTIVE. Remember to give your character a specific goal.

4. Characters often have three wants: Original, Developing and Ending.

5. There are four types of character arcs: Positive, Negative, No-Change-Tragic and No-Change-Superhero.

6. Much-needed complexity can be added by lightening up the villain or darkening up the hero.

7. Characters are either Static (do not change) or Dynamic (they do change).

8. To create a realistic/full character arc, flesh out the Old Self to New Self Steps: Old Self → Struggling Self → Emerging Self → Last Big Decision → New Self.

9. Finding your character's wound can help you better understand and articulate what motivates/drives your character's actions.

10. Uncovering your character's archetype can give your character depth, weight and mass identifiability.

TOOL #4

Defining the SHAPE of Your Story

What You Have Done So Far

Tool #1: By figuring out where you write best, how you write best and by creating a nurturing place to write, you have given yourself the best chance at writing success.

Tool #2: By working to craft a solid story idea and theme, you have laid a strong foundation upon which to build your story.

Tool #3: By traveling through the 9 Character Elements, you have added compelling characters to your creative stew.

Now it is time to learn a little about how to *shape* your story.

"I'm Blind, I Tell You, I'm Blind!"

This is how it went down. I was a young and stupid writer—but oh, filled with so many ideas. I was writing one of my first screenplays and I wasn't sure where the story was going. My brain was filled with so many possibilities and they all seemed right. Plus, I couldn't decide which moments of the story went where. So, one of my insightful teachers hooked me up with an accomplished writing mentor and we began meeting weekly. Her name was Song-Glory, or Sunny-Light or Song-Light, I can't remember. She was beautiful, calm and sweet, born and raised in Santa Cruz. And that girl could write. We would meet under a big oak tree. Anyway, on one cloudy afternoon, this conversation took place:

"How is your story going this week, Marni?"

"I'm pretty sure I'm lost."

"Ohhhh, I bet you're not. I bet if you just trust your intuition, it will lead you in the right direction."

"Trust my intuition?"

"Yeah, try it."

So, I went home and did my best to trust my intuition. I meditated. I sat and stared at a crystal. (Yeah, I had no idea where to find my intuition; it wasn't in the crystal.) I thought I finally found some intuition, but it just seemed to give me some more cool things I wanted to write about. I still couldn't figure out the right order. Back to the mentor, back to the oak tree.

"Okay now, for sure, I'm lost. I don't know where to put parts of the story."

"Marni, you're not lost. You're right where you're supposed to be. Just travel into your heart."

"How do you do that?"

"Well, you can use your third eye."

"Huh?"

"Your third eye, you know. Try thinking of it as a 'meta' organ that consists of all of your senses plus your mind. And when they work together they can create a bigger, more powerful sensory organ. Just imagine your third eye, then travel inward and you'll see the path." She was so confident. She made it sound so simple.

"Ummm, okay."

Home I went, and I sat on my stupid hard bed and tried to find a way to get into my third eye so I could find my heart and/or my intuition, which I had been told would surely know the way. Twenty minutes into the meditation, I threw my shoe across the room. Back to the oak tree.

"I need tools. I'm lost and I need tools."

"Did you try using your intuition?"

"Yes."

"Did you try using your third eye?

"Yeah, it turns out I'm totally blind in my third eye."

She laughed. "Okay, so what do you think you need?"

"I need to see it visually. What is the shape of a story? I need to see the shape of a story so I can begin to think of where to put things."

"Oh, why didn't you just say so?" She took out a pen and paper and drew something that resembled this:

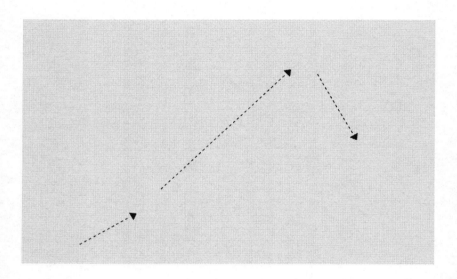

I looked it over. I took the drawing home and studied it. And the shape of my story began to get clear. If I could figure out the climax and the ending, then I knew where I was headed. And if I knew where I was headed, then I could go backward and fill in the rest.

Within an hour, the story unfolded in front of my eyes.

(By the way, I'm in no way disparaging the use of the third eye or following your gut or heart. But sometimes, a simple drawing helps.)

When I sit down to work with a writer, I start by drawing them this diagram.

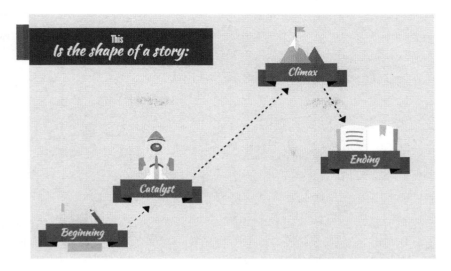

Yes, there are several more points to know about your story, but I figured out that you must *at least* know these 3 Essential KEY Spots to uncover the basic shape of your story. Let's define the 3 Key Spots:

Ending: How your story concludes. What happens to the protagonist? Does he or doesn't he reach his goal? Is it a happy, sad or bittersweet ending?

Climax: What is the highest moment of tension → the peak of conflict for your story? How do the protagonist and the antagonist meet for a final face-off? How does the protagonist face his biggest fear, flaw or conflict?

Catalyst: What event launches the story? What is the call to action for our protagonist? What moment starts the protagonist on the climb up the mountain?

Q: Why is it so important to know these 3 Key Spots?

A: These 3 Key Spots create the basic mountain shape that all great stories possess. The protagonist is called into action, has a goal of some sort and the tension rises until a climax. After the climax, there's an ending or a resolution.

Q: What if I want to know more plot points? NOW?!

A: Hold your horses. We will elaborate more and create a more detailed map of your story in Tool #5. But knowing these three elements first will greatly assist you in creating a story with a strong shape and compelling narrative. So chill out.

Q: Where do most writers struggle?

A: Most writers struggle with the climax. Usually, this stems from the problem that they have made their protagonist inactive—or left him/her without a goal. A protagonist with a goal has a fairly identifiable climax. It is the moment he faces the evil beast and either does or does not meet his goal.

Some writers struggle with the ending. They don't want to think about the ending before they write. They want to "write to find it." This is one way to go. Just prepare to be open to many rewrites to make sure your story flows and makes sense.

I encourage writers to know their ending because it gives them a clear path. It's the destination on the map. If a pirate wants to get to the gold, he needs to know where the big "X" is on the map. He needs to know his destination. So it is for writers. The ones who don't know their destination tend to wander and meander, and that kind of writing can be difficult to read.

Do You Know These Five Guys?

(Just so you can sound like you know what you're talking about at a dinner party.) These five guys helped us to better understand the essentials of story shape.

Aristotle (384 B.C.–322 B.C.) was a Greek philosopher and student of Plato. He was arguably the world's first literary and theatrical scholar. Over 2,000 years ago, in *Poetics*, he instructed that "A whole is what has a beginning and middle and end." (Technically: a protasis, epitasis and a catastrophe.) This is the basic "Three-Act Structure" of dramatic storytelling, and Aristotle's influences are felt to this day.

Horace (65 B.C.–8 B.C.) was a celebrated Roman poet/drama critic. Sometimes called the "Roman Aristotle," he wrote *Ars Poetica* (The Art of Playwriting), a set of rules for writing drama based on Aristotle's *Poetics*. Horace made a big impact on modern dramatists and supported the Five-Act Structure: "Neue minor neu sit quinto productior actu fibula," lines 189–190 ("A play should not be shorter or longer than five acts"). He's attributed with the notion of dropping the audience into the action, called in medias res ("into the middle of things").

Lucius Annaeus Seneca (4 B.C.–65 A.D.) The Roman philosopher-poet Lucius Annaeus Seneca developed Senecan Tragedy. He wrote nine plays that were probably intended to be recited rather than performed on stage. They were written in five acts with intervening choruses and bloodthirsty plots including crimes, sometimes called revenge tragedies. The conventional Five-Act Structure of Renaissance drama owes its origin to Seneca.

Shakespeare (1564–1616) Arguably the world's greatest dramatist, he wrote his plays in five acts. The Elizabethan Five-Act Structure evolved from the Greek form and remains an often-used starting point for contemporary films and plays.

Gustav Freytag (1816–1895) a German novelist, playwright and story master and the author of *Die Technik des Dramas*, a theory of dramatic structure that also advocated the Five-Act Structure. It was later known as Freytag's Pyramid. It stinks that he was a blatant racist whose novels contributed to racism in his homeland; nevertheless, he did contribute to our thinking here. According to Freytag, the plot of a story is broken up into five acts: exposition, rising action, climax, falling action and resolution/catastrophe.

Five-Act Structure

1. **Exposition.** Can also be called the introduction. It is the initial section and provides the reader with the background information that is necessary to follow and comprehend the rest of the story. It is also the place where the main problem of the story is introduced, thus engaging or hooking the audience's attention.

2. **Rising Action.** Initial conflict becomes complicated by secondary conflicts. Obstacles are placed in front of the protagonist—he simply cannot reach his goal. The antagonist makes trouble along with lesser adversaries. The tension escalates and the stakes get higher.

3. **Climax.** The most dramatic moment also called the turning point. This turning point marks a change for the protagonist for the better or worse. In a comedy → life has gone poorly, but now things are starting to look up. In a tragedy → life has gone well for the protagonist, but now things are going poorly.

4. **Falling Action.** Conflict between the protagonist and antagonist unfolds. The protagonist will either win or lose here. May include the final suspenseful moment. The climax is over and now we want to understand how it will all be resolved.

5. **Resolution, Denouement** or **Catastrophe.** This is the conclusion of the story. The events between the falling action and the end of the story. The main conflict is resolved here. A release of tension occurs. A new normal exists for the protagonist. In a comedy → the protagonist is better off than where he started. In a tragedy → the protagonist experiences a catastrophe and is worse off than where he started.

Q: What exactly is a denouement?

A: A French word derived from the Old French word *desnoer*, which means, "to untie" and from *nodus*, which is Latin for "knot." So literally, it is untying the knot. You know, the moment when the answer to the mystery (or the question in the story) is revealed.

Q: Why don't we use the Five-Act Structure anymore?

A: Over the last 100 years, we have moved back to more of a Three-Act Structure. Ibsen and other playwrights took the medium toward the model we use today.

Okay, 'nuff history. Now back to Tool #4 →

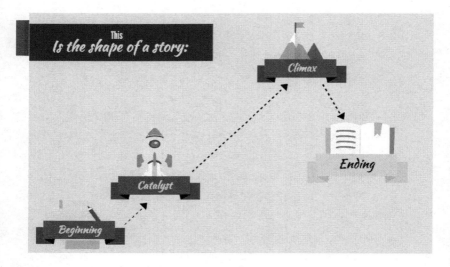

Key Spot #1: The Ending

Often in a session with a writer who hasn't fully decided on his idea, we will discuss the ending first. Once we know where we are headed, we can then go backward and bring the characters to that inevitable moment.

Q: What do I do if I don't know the ending?

A: I will answer this question in two parts.

Part 1: In my opinion, most writers know their stories even if they don't think they do. If you are not sure, use the "take-a-guess" method. It's the easiest tool out there. Try taking a guess by just tossing out some ideas about the ending. You can be wrong and you can change your mind. But chances are you do know the ending—it's just lurking in your brain, waiting for you to have some confidence in it.

Part 2: If you really don't know your ending, (although, I still contest that you do!) then I suggest you do some writing exercises to find it. I know, I've said it before, but I'm nagging you for your own good. You will want to know your end before you start writing. Otherwise, it's like taking a trip with no destination in mind. This is a fun idea for a day trip, but not so good for writing something as complicated as a novel, play or screenplay. Writers who have tackled their first drafts without knowing the ending have written me the following:

"It's a hot mess; the story goes this way and that way, and the whole piece doesn't hang together. It's almost like two stories in one. I'm just not sure what makes sense and what doesn't."

"I wish I took the time to think through the ending before I began. I could have plotted it out and written it once. Now, I'm in rewriting hell."

"I liked the idea of just writing and finding out where it was going. The problem was that it was going in so many directions that while people liked my writing style, they had trouble following the story itself."

When you know the end, you often know the beginning and the middle (and other places too). The beginning, middle and ending are all points on the arc of your story—they're connected. Knowing the end often reveals the other parts. Here are some simple points to illustrate this idea:

1. The ending point is often the opposing moment from the midpoint.

- Example: Let's take a traditional boy-meets-girl story. But, I know you—you're a rebel and you want an example that isn't trite. So let's make this love story a tragedy. Let's name the guy Jake. In the beginning, Jake is lonely yet hopeful. Then he meets Cherie, an amazing girl, his soulmate, and he does everything in his power to get her. At the end, Jake does not get Cherie, and he has given up on love.

2. If the ending is positive or happy (an up note), then the middle is usually a down note.

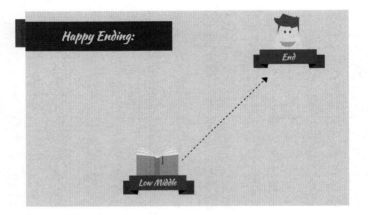

- If we were writing a traditional Hollywood rom-com, then in the middle it would look like they'll never end up together (and yet, in the end, beating all the odds, somehow they do).

3. If the ending is negative or tragic (a down note), then the middle is usually an up note.

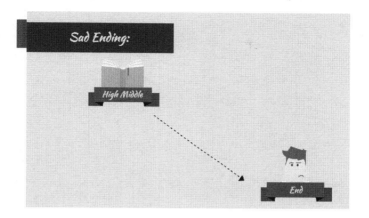

- Example: Let's continue with our non-traditional boy-meets-girl story. Even though they're meant to be together, at the end of our story Jake is left alone and bereft. So in the middle, Jake and Cherie are happily together (or at least things look pretty damn good for them).

Note: Above all else → you have to remain true to the nature of your particular story. These are guidelines, not absolutes.

Here are some examples of how the ending impacts—or is a reflection of—the beginning and the middle:

The Wizard of Oz
Beginning: Dorothy is running away from home, she doesn't believe in her own power.
Middle: Trying to get home, fears she will never make it back.
End: Returning home, now appreciating home and loved ones and believing in her own power.

The Godfather
Beginning: Michael wants nothing to do with his family business.
Middle: He is going to escape the pull of the mobster life.
End: He is the new Godfather.

Romeo and Juliet
Beginning: The star-crossed lovers meet. It's love at first sight.
Middle: They will do anything to be with one another. They make a plan—there is hope.
End: They are both dead, neither one wanting to live without the other.

What Makes a Good Ending?

You don't need an ending that is happy.

You don't need an ending that is shocking or wildly clever.

You don't need an ending that is all wrapped up with a pretty bow.

You need an ending that is satisfying.

I can hear you thinking. You are wondering: *How do I do that?* Well, let's muse a little bit about what makes an ending satisfying.

An ending is satisfying because the writer took the reader on an amazing journey.

An ending is satisfying because, while on the journey, the reader was unsure if or how the protagonist would get out of trouble.

An ending is satisfying when we realize that the soul of the character or the soul of the society has been challenged to its very core.

An ending is satisfying when there is an elegant twist (all the clues were there, we just hadn't looked at in that way before).

Happy Ending: It was hoped for, sought after, cried over and fought for—but it was unsure. There was a ride to get there, filled with twists and turns.

Sad/Tragic Ending: This type of ending was hard fought, so the loss is painful.

Through the eyes of the protagonist, we have struggled for this ending and it is our victory or our defeat as well. That's satisfying.

Examples of Well-done Endings

Romeo and Juliet (by Shakespeare): Romeo and Juliet's parents find their dead bodies. They decide to bury the hatchet in the interest of peace.

One Flew Over the Cuckoo's Nest (by Ken Kesey): The once brash and rebellious McMurphy is reunited with the rest of the patients after his lobotomy. The Chief sees that he is in a vegetative state—not speaking or moving—and nearly dead. Late that night, in an act of compassion, the Chief smothers McMurphy with a pillow. He then throws the shower-room control panel (planted in an early scene as crazy heavy) through the window, running from the hospital to freedom.

Rocky (The first one! By Sylvester Stallone.): While he doesn't win the fight, he gets into the ring and goes the distance. He wins self-respect and self-confidence that will change his life forever.

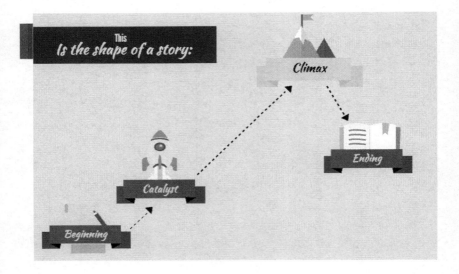

Key Spot #2: The Climax

After a writer knows their ending, we then work on the climax. For our purposes here, we will be considering the climax as the very last confrontation between the protagonist and antagonist, or **the highest peak of conflict**. So, working backward, we know where the writer wants to end their piece. We know who wins. So the climax is simply the final battle between the two forces.

Note: The forces can be internal or external.

Q: Where does the climax occur?

A: Very, very, very close to the end. Some say it is only a few pages from the last page of the book. The reason it occurs so close to the end is that once the climax occurs, the tension is gone, the mystery is solved and the reader is more or less satisfied. The only thing left to do is to wrap up the story.

Writing Tips: The climax should be the most exciting or dramatic moment of your story. Make sure to utilize all the excitement by increasing your reader's anticipation of this moment → build up to it.

Often, great climaxes are paired with a "last-big-decision" moment. One of my students calls it a "One-two punch."

Last-Big-Decision Moment: A moment when the character is faced with a decision—to stay in his old ways (Old Self) or to face his flaw and try being his New Self (to act with courage, strength, belief, hope, etc.). Usually, this decision leads to a revelation. This revelation might inform the protagonist how to best conquer the antagonist.

Opportunity for Originality: Every climax is unique. It must be a result of the protagonist's journey. Let your imagination run wild here. There are many fun and inventive ways to show the highest peak of conflict.

Examples of Well-done Climaxes

The Lord of the Rings Trilogy (J.R.R. Tolkien, films in 2001–2003)
When Frodo makes that life-changing decision not to destroy the Ring. This is evidence that the Ring is much too powerful for any hobbit or human being to have in their possession.

It's a Wonderful Life (Directed by Frank Capra, 1947)
After George has experienced the world without him in it, he runs back to the bridge and prays to live again. This leads to the highest peak of conflict when the town rallies to help George make up the lost money before he is arrested.

Titanic (Directed by James Cameron, 1997)
When Rose decides not to stay in the lifeboat but to rejoin Jack on the Titanic. She has made the decision of love over her life.

Now we have two key pieces of information: Where the protagonist ends up (ending) and how he ends up this way (climax). At this point, let's travel back to the beginning and select the catalyst → the moment the protagonist received the call to head up the mountain.

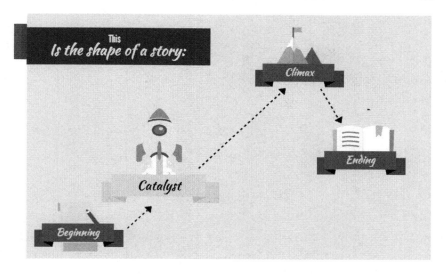

Key Spot #3: The Catalyst

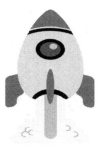

What is a catalyst? The catalyst is a call to action. The protagonist is being lured out of his Old World and into a new one where his flaws will be challenged and his fears must be faced. *Come on, protagonist—it's time to go up the mountain.*

Opportunity for Originality: Think of your story. How do you expect your catalyst to happen? How can you craft a catalyst moment that you've never seen? (Sometimes it's the opposite of what you expect to happen.)

Q: Where does the catalyst occur in the story?

A: The catalyst occurs early on in your story, usually after we know some basic and important information about the current life situation of our protagonist.

Examples of Well-done Catalyst Moments

Jurassic Park (Directed by Steven Spielberg, 1993)
Scientists Grant and Ellie need money to continue funding their research. Hammond enters and asks for Grant and Ellie's help to assess his "biological preserve" in Costa Rica. He says there is a problem with the project and the people who are funding the venture are getting nervous and need reassurance. Grant and Ellie initially turn him down, but Hammond persists, offering to fund their research for three years. They happily accept. Time to go up the mountain.

The Avengers (Directed by Joss Whedon, 2012)
Loki (the god of mischief) is causing tremendous damage to Earth and must be stopped. Nick Fury sets out on a mission to reactivate the Avengers Initiative, traveling to each superhero to call them back into action, for only as a team can they hope to beat Loki and save the planet.

The Help (Directed by Tate Taylor, 2011)
Skeeter is a young journalist who notices the injustices being experienced by the black maids who serve the white women in Jackson, Mississippi, in 1963. Skeeter wants to bring their plight to the light of day and asks a maid, Aibileen, to help her do just that.

The Hunger Games (Directed by Gary Ross, 2012)
Prim, Katniss's little sister, is the unlucky girl tribute chosen for the Hunger Games. Katniss volunteers to take her place and protect her sister.

DID YOU KNOW?

Jo-ha-kyū 序破急

Jo-ha-kyū is a concept of modulation and movement that has been applied to a wide variety of traditional Japanese arts. Roughly translated to "beginning, break, rapid," it essentially means that all actions should start slowly, speed up and then end swiftly.

Walking Through the "3 Key Spots" Process With a Writer

Remember: Paul's Full Story Idea
Nick, a playboy heir and low-level scientist, gets a job in a government lab purely out of nepotism. Underestimated by everyone, Nick uncovers the lab's horrific secret, that his boss is actually a dangerous bioterrorist bent on selling a deadly toxin to an enemy country. Nick must face his lack of courage, his less-than-stellar reputation and his mentally twisted boss in order to stop the diabolical plans to kill thousands of innocent people.

Step 1: Finding the Ending
Paul wanted his hero to experience selflessness for the first time in his life. Paul felt that Nick's story was of a man who had been given everything in the world and yet hated himself—mostly because he had never learned the value of giving.

Paul's Ending: Nick has risked everything despite the fact that no one will ever know what he has done. Though the world still views him as a lazy playboy, in the last 24 hours he nearly died as he took down his twisted boss in order to save the people of Washington, D.C., from being exposed to the deadly toxin.

Step 2: Finding the Climax
So now, working backward, we know that the climax is the highest point of conflict. It is where good vs. evil duke it out and only one can win. The climax often asks a question. In this case, the question is: Will Nick find his courage and save the city from the deadly toxin?

Paul's Climax: Nick risks his life by breaking into the lab just as his boss is about to sell the toxin. He outsmarts his boss, steals the toxin and takes a serious beating. He barely escapes with his life and gets the toxin safely into the hands of the authorities.

Knowing the climax is nothing to sneeze at. Meaning, it is a VERY BIG DEAL! If you know the climax, then you know that everything from the catalyst forward is an uphill climb toward the climax.

So now, Paul knows that he must keep all the action moving up toward the moment when Nick confronts his boss face to face.

Step 3: Finding the Catalyst
Now, to continue working backward, we travel waayyyyyy back to the beginning, to Act 1 and the call to action, the catalyst. Paul asked himself: *What would make Nick have to face his completely lazy, self-centered way of living?* He came up with this:

Paul's Catalyst: Nick has been hired on at the lab, and it has been made clear to him that he is to keep his head down and stay away from the "important work" that the real scientists are doing. At first he is happy to check in, do a half-assed job and continue his life as a party boy. The catalyst occurs when he discovers that something is not right about the lab—in fact, his boss may be part of something extremely dangerous. By learning this information, he can no longer continue to live the life he has led; he must start the climb up the mountain toward facing his greatest fears and flaws.

Ready to try it out yourself?

Story Shape Worksheet

The 3 Key Spots of My Story

My Catalyst is:

_____

_____

_____

_____

My Climax is:

_____

_____

_____

_____

My Ending is:

_____

_____

_____

_____

Takeaway Lessons for Tool #4 Defining the SHAPE of Your Story

1. There are 3 Key Spots that will help you define the BASIC SHAPE of your story. These Spots are: catalyst, climax and ending. These three points create the basic mountain shape that all great stories possess. It's often helpful to travel backward when creating a story:

   Key Spot #1: Ending—How your story concludes. What happens to the protagonist? Does he or doesn't he reach his goal? Is it a happy, sad or bittersweet ending?
   Key Spot #2: Climax—What is the highest moment of tension → the peak of conflict for your story? How do the protagonist and the antagonist meet for a final face off? How does the protagonist face his biggest flaw, fear or conflict?
   Key Spot #3: Catalyst—The call to action. The protagonist is being lured out of her old world and into her new one, where her flaws will be challenged and her fears must be faced. *Come on, protagonist—it's time to go up the mountain!*

2. Most writers struggle with the climax. Mostly, that's because their protagonist is inactive—or has no clear (specific) goal. A protagonist with a specific goal has a fairly definable climax. It is the moment he faces the evil beast and either does or does not meet his goal.

3. Last-Big-Decision Moment = a moment close to the climax when the character is faced with a decision—to stay in her old ways (Old Self) or to face her flaw and try being her New Self (to act with courage, strength, belief, hope, etc.). Usually, this decision leads to a revelation. This revelation might inform the protagonist how best to conquer the antagonist.

4. The best endings don't have to be happy or pretty-bow-perfect, but they do have to be satisfying.

TOOL #5

PLOT AND POUR
Structure for Everything From Novels to Memoirs

"Writing a novel is like heading out over the open sea in a small boat. It helps if you have a plan and a course laid out." —John Gardner

What You Have Done So Far

Tool #1: By figuring out where you write best, how you write best and by creating a nurturing place to write, you have given yourself the best chance at writing success.

Tool #2: By working to craft a solid story idea and theme, you have laid a strong foundation upon which to build your story.

Tool #3: By traveling through the 9 Character Elements, you have added compelling characters to your creative stew.

Tool #4: By learning the 3 Key Spots, you have given your story a basic shape.

Now it's time to learn a little about how to flesh out the story.

The Incident

Here's how I remember "the incident." I'm in the dreary, square classroom at the USC School of Filmic Writing and my teacher is a drill sergeant. A literal drill sergeant. He's got a flat top; his face is all red and he's in my face. Yelling. "Where's your inciting incident?! It's supposed to be on page three! Where is your #*!*ing inciting incident?"

Then I yell back, in front of all the other students who are staring in horror, "It's not on page three! It will never be on page three!" Then we stare each other down for a long, tense moment, neither one backing down. Until he says, "When and if you stop resisting structure, your writing will take off."

The reality was probably far less dramatic, but that's how that scene plays out in my brain. Why is it stuck there so permanently in my noggin? Is it because I listened to him? Hell, no. I fought the man for years. Structure was a bitch, and I had no care for it.

But the drill sergeant was right. And I learned that lesson a short decade later.

So, bottom line—skip a decade of fighting something you will ultimately embrace in one fashion or another.

Q: So, it's all about plotting?

A: I think you know the answer to that one. (No.) It's jumping back and forth—plot when you can and pour when you need to.

Let's define a bit.

Plot: Your story idea laid out into a structure. How the events unfold. What specific events happen to take us from start to finish?

Do the plotting work—it sucks, but it works. Think it through—it's going to give you parameters.

And there's good news—you are closer than you think. Sure, you have to know 15 Plot Spots, but you already know three of them (ending, climax and catalyst), so you just have 12 more to go.

Pour: The process where you imagine turning on the tap in your mind and let the story speak to you—tell you where it wants to go. Getting everything in your head down on the page without censoring or analyzing.

Q: So, when do I plot and when do I pour?

A: In an ideal world—well, at least in my ideal world—a writer would spend months creating a clever, rich and deep plot outline from beginning to end in full detail. Then, and only then, would the writer sit down at the page (or the computer) for that all-important first draft. During which, of course, the writer would follow the outline perfectly from one plot point to the next. Then, even if imperfect, the writer would have a nicely plotted first draft.

HOWEVER, Phil, a great writer in one of my ongoing writing groups, pointed out that sometimes—oftentimes—the story comes from just allowing any and all information to pour out. Sometimes, to find the story, you have to follow the pen. HOWEVER, sometimes when you follow the pen for too long, you can come out with a mountain of meandering pages. Then the task becomes taking the already written pages and trying to stuff them into a workable structure (which can be supremely painful in a variety of ways).

So—How to solve this conundrum?

After watching how writers plan, brainstorm, write and rewrite for 20 years, here's what I have come up with:

1. Create two notebooks or files; one for planning your plot and one for pouring (information dumping).

2. Start with the planning notebook. Plan as much as you can before you write. For some, this will be one page, for others, 20 pages or more.

3. If you get stuck, or if inspiration is calling you in a certain direction, pour it out in your "information-dump" notebook. A nicer way to put it is that **you can balance your planning sessions with "finding your story" sessions.**

Oh, and you want some good news?

STARING OUT THE WINDOW COUNTS!

When you are in the planning stages, spend time daydreaming—you will find you will have more to pour.

4. After you information-dump, when you have found out what your story has to tell you, return to your planning notebook and incorporate this new information into your outline.

5. Do this as long as you can stand it before starting your first draft.

This—I believe—is a nice, happy medium between guiding your story and letting your story (or the muse or inspiration or the creative process) guide you.

Note: All writers have a different tolerance for structure and planning. In order to keep writing and to ultimately finish your first draft, you must find the method that works for you. Be willing to experiment and try out new methods. I firmly believe that every writer has an effective writing practice within them, if only they stay with the process long enough to uncover it. Now let the dance begin.

15 Plot Spots!

1. The Grabber
2. Old Self in Old World
3. This Changes Everything/The Catalyst
4. Struggles and Prep
5. Here We Go
6. Rough Landing/Small Victories
7. The Gut (Middle)
8. Do a Little Dance/Danger Looming
9. Revelation and/or Obstacle
10. The Mini Crisis
11. New Self Emerging
12. It's Not Looking Good
13. Last Big Decision: Old vs. New Self
14. Climax
15. The Wrap Up: The Ending

A Little Reminder of What We Can Learn From Pirates:

Pirates know exactly what they want: treasure. And, in general, (as stated previously, I'm sort of a pirate expert), most pirates don't like to wander around aimlessly in search of said treasure.

Generally, **pirates carry a map.** A map with a big red "X." Smart thinking. They know what they want, and they have instructions to get it.

Pirates are not afraid to be who they are. They curse and spit and say what's on their mind. They let it all hang out.

A good writer (and a good pirate) is one who

- Knows where they are headed.
- Has some sort of map.
- Is willing to be authentic, to let it all hang out.

Okay, enough about pirates.

ATTENTION, STRUCTURE-RESISTANT WRITERS:

The Biggest Mistake Writers Make Is: Writing Too Soon

Now, you may be wondering what the heck I mean by "writing too soon." Well, I'm gonna school ya. And I'm going to start by sharing what I consider to be "Beginning-Writer's Attitude" and "Advanced-Writer's Attitude." See if you can locate yourself in either of these categories.

Beginning-Writer's Attitude sounds like this:

> *"I'm only accomplishing something when I'm putting words on the page."*
>
> *"I'm a free-flow kind of writer, and structure inhibits my creativity."*
>
> *"I'm not trying to make stupid commercial work; I'm making high art."* (*Note:* High art is well structured.)
>
> *"I'm not a formula kind of writer. I'm an original thinker."*
>
> *"I'm really busy and all that preplanning is a waste of my actual writing time."*

Advanced-Writer's Attitude sounds like this:

> "Prewriting—or how I plan out my story—is a huge accomplishment."

> "Even though I'm not churning out copy, I'm saving myself from throwing away this first draft entirely or rewriting it over and over again."

> "The more I outline and prewrite until I'm satisfied, the stronger my storytelling will be."

> "I will not go to the page until I'm really confident about my outline and I can't wait to get to my computer!"

Now, I fully understand Beginning-Writer's Attitude. Why? Because I had adopted that attitude myself for years. I was a real artist: I would not be formulaic or be stuffed into a box. However, I kept getting the same feedback: "Great writer, but it doesn't come together at the end."

Finally, I got fed up and decided I wanted to sell, make a living and display mastery of the craft. And so I began to embrace structure. It's not easy, but sometimes you've just got to suck it up and realize that your thinking may not be helping you to grow as a writer. Prewriting often doesn't feel all that great because you are not churning out copy. It's not as tangible as printing out pages and holding them in your hands. And truth be told, looking at cards on your wall or reworking an outline until it feels ready can be downright annoying. However, there are big consequences to writing without an outline.

The main problem is trying to apply structure to a draft that's already written. This is troublesome because it's not as easy to see a clear and clean through-line if you have to slog through hundreds of pages. But the real problem is that once the writer has committed to the words on the page, they are far, far, far less willing to move sections around or eliminate them altogether. Trust me on this. Writers will always tell me, "I don't have a problem with rewriting," or "I don't mind moving scenes around," but when it gets down to it, they resist change at every turn.

Here is the best description I have ever heard or read about when describing the need to plan and outline before writing. It comes from Rob Tobin, author of *How to Write High Structure, High Concept Movies*.

"My main advice is to outline the material completely before starting to write the first draft. Think of it like firing a gun at a target a hundred feet away. If the barrel of the gun is off a fraction of an inch, the bullet will actually miss the target by several inches or even feet, because the error gets magnified over time and distance. If you do not have your story's structure down, any mistakes you make in that structure at the beginning will expand over the course of the story, and it will be huge by the time you've finished that story. In fact the error might even prevent you from finishing the story. I used to be a development exec; I've read and closely analyzed thousands upon thousands of screenplays. Almost all errors are structural if you follow them back far enough. They all have to do with the barrel of the gun being 'off' just so slightly (and sometimes not so slightly) and that 'offness' magnifying over the course of the story."

The good news here is that all it takes to advance as a writer is a shift in attitude, and that can be done at any moment that you choose.

Remember: You can fight the law, but wouldn't you rather just be a great writer? If too much structure stops you from writing altogether, then find where your comfort level lies. What I have found is that writers tend to get more comfortable with structure over time. So start where you can, and if you can increase to more structure, then push yourself a teensy bit.

REASONS TO OUTLINE YOUR PLOT

1. You have a road map. If you outline, you will know what to write first. And when you are done writing what comes first, magically, you will know what to write next.

2. You will save time. You won't waste time staring at the screen wondering what to write that day. This is especially vital when you are pressed for writing time. If you have a half hour or an hour to write, then every minute of writing time will count.

3. You can see the weak spots visually. By looking at your outline, you will be able to see the holes in your story and the areas where your characters are weak, as well as the areas that are solid.

Outlining will highlight

- Holes in the character arc
- Holes in the plot
- Areas that need deepening
- Areas that need strengthening

4. You are more willing to change your work during the outlining stage. Once writers commit their ideas to the page, they are seriously reluctant to make changes. When I say *seriously reluctant* I mean: *They don't want to make the changes.* It's called "But-I've-already-written-it-this-way-itis." For many writers, changing what they have written is like rewriting the Bible. Think of it this way: During the outline stage, making a huge change like, say, making the main character a woman instead of a man may happen with a shrug. It may be uncomfortable to make the change, but it won't be painful. When you have written six chapters, and you have realized that your novel would work sooo much better if your main character were a woman, you would probably resist the change at every turn, even if you knew it was the right move.

5. It's a learning tool. You will learn a tremendous amount about your story as a living beast. You will also learn a lot about yourself as a writer. Areas of strength and weakness will become clear. *Note:* An outline is NOT the Ten Commandments. In other words, you can put a few ideas down, and the next day you can change your mind.

Q: Will my outline change?

A: Most likely, yes.

As you plot, it will affect what you pour out.

As you pour it out, that will affect what you plot.

I call it course correction.

Your outline will not be perfect; it will most likely have holes and imperfections. But get as much down as is humanly possible. Give it your best shot. That's it. **Be a Solution-Focused Writer.** As you outline, you WILL discover holes, inconsistencies and areas of weakness. It's just the nature of the beast. As you come up against each problem, tell yourself the solution is right around the corner.

In other words, EXPECT to encounter problematic issues and EXPECT to find their solutions.

Then, let it go and allow it to come to you as you go about your day. Often the ideas come to you as you walk, as you shower, as you exercise, as you drive. Don't lose faith—the idea will come.

"*A rule says, 'You must do it this way.' A principle says, 'This works... and it has through all remembered time.' The difference is crucial. Your work needn't be modeled after the 'well made' play; rather it must be well made within the principles that shape our art. Anxious, inexperienced writers obey rules. Rebellious, unschooled writers break rules. Artists master the form.*" —Robert McKee, author of *Story*

Okay, time to get acquainted with the 15 Essential Plot Spots.

15 Essential Plot Spots

This is a plotting tool that can be used for movies, plays, memoirs and novels. Here are a few notes to help you with the tool:

Your Story's Logic

Always be aware of the logic of your story. Every story has its own logic and integrity. Use this plotting tool as a guideline. Feel free to add or subtract in areas that make sense for your story.

Moments and Sequences

Some Plot Spots work better as Moments—single events or specific beats to hit. Then again, some Plot Spots work better as Sequences, which consist of a series of moments and events.

- Moments will be coded as (M).
- Sequences will be coded as (S).

If the Plot Spot can be a moment or a sequence (author's choice), it will be coded as (M or S).

Revelations and Obstacles

Revelation: A new piece of information that comes to light or when the character thinks of a new option or conclusion.

Obstacles: Roadblocks, interference or disruption of your protagonist along his or her path. Anything that gets in the way of your protagonist's progress.

Both revelations and obstacles will be found throughout your plot. You may find yourself placing a revelation or an obstacle (or both) in between the designated 15 Plot Spots. You can always ask the question: *What does the story need?* Then, let that guide where you place important revelations and obstacles.

Writing Tip: Use a revelation/obstacle to create tension or in some way UP the climb toward the climax. According to the logic of your story, you can select just one revelation or obstacle or many. The most important aspect is that the revelation or obstacle raises the stakes or UPS THE CONFLICT toward the climax.

15 Essential Plot Spots

1. The Grabber:
First page to first five pages (M or S, Usually M)
- Do something interesting and do it quick.
- Hook us.
- Grab us and tell us why we should get involved in this world.

2. Old Self in Old World:
1st Quarter of the Story. ACT 1 continues here. (S)
- Introduction of protagonist's Old Self → fears, flaws, weaknesses, desires and needs. Highlight protagonist's flaws that he/she will need to face. Show don't tell.

- Protagonist's Original Want → most of the time the protagonist wants to avoid change.
- Bond us to the protagonist → why do we love or care about the protagonist? Or, what makes the protagonist compelling to watch?
- Introduction of the Old World → set the stage: Where and when does the story take place? Who are the surrounding major characters? How are they living? What kind of conflict is happening in the Old World? (What is not working in the Old World?)
- Leave Us Curious → not too much backstory if you can help it.
- Identify the Evil Beast(s) → an external element (antagonist, part of society) and/or an internal element (part of self) that needs fixing.

3. This Changes Everything/The Catalyst: at 10-15%
Early on in beginning section. ACT 1 continues here. (M or S, usually M)
- The event that launches the journey.
- The knock on the door, the call to adventure.
- Old Self is challenged to start looking into the possibility of becoming the New Self.
- Start the rising action here.

Note: Some stories call for the catalyst to be placed in between two sections of Old Self in Old World. So the structure looks like: The Grabber, A Bit of Old Self in Old World, The Catalyst and More Old Self in Old World.

4. Struggles and Prep:
The aftermath of the catalyst (S). In this section the protagonist may:
- <u>Struggle with the journey</u>: The protagonist wonders whether or not to go on the journey or enter the New World. "Should I take the call?" The protagonist may express positive or negative thoughts/feelings about the information presented in the

catalyst. If the protagonist is running from the journey, they may be trying to stay entrenched in old ways (even though the need for a change may be obvious). Think: denial, anger, reluctance, hiding, rejecting the journey, rejecting the need to change.
- <u>Prepare for the journey</u>: If and when the protagonist decides to go on the journey, the next step is for them to meet with the mentor/wise person for training, advice and to get supplies for the journey.

Note: Often, the protagonist runs from the journey, then prepares for it.

--- **End ACT 1** ---

--- **ACT 2 Begins Here** ---

5. Here We Go: at 25%
We are leaving ACT 1; ACT 2 begins. The end of the beginning. (M)
- The protagonist launches himself into a new world; journey begins.
- The protagonist often has a new, specific want or goal: Developing Want. (Protagonist is on a mission.)
- The conflict and/or tension is real and present.
- The action has begun to rise.

6. Rough Landing/Small Victories:
Beginning of the middle section. (S)
After the protagonist has a goal, has walked through the door into the New World and launches himself into the journey, he will experience some Small Victories (initial success) or a Rough Landing—or a little of both.
- <u>Rough Landing</u> → people may not like the protagonist in the New World; he is a stranger in a strange land. Encountering

small moments of defeat, tests, and enemies often makes the audience want the protagonist to get in there and fight.
- Small Victories → the protagonist may experience some initial success and may think it's going to be a piece of cake in the New World. They may actually have a lot of fun initially, sometimes encountering tests, allies and enemies but sailing through. These small moments of victory may give the protagonist bits of confidence, thinking they can ace the journey.

Note: Whether it's a rough landing or a small victory, in the New World the protagonist will encounter tests, allies and enemies. The protagonist may develop a new mini-goal based on their overall goal.

7. The Gut: at 50% (Middle of Your Story)
Smack in the middle of ACT 2/Midpoint. (M or S, Usually M)
- Hit us in the gut.
- Often in a comedy (or when there is happy ending) the Midpoint is a false defeat. Think → Old Self is winning.
- Often in a tragedy or sad ending, the Midpoint is a false victory where the New Self is winning.
- Protagonist has lost hope or is on top of the world.
- In some cases, the story makes a dramatic shift, as if the first half of the story and the second half are distinct from one another.
- Keep the tension up and the conflict rising.

8. Do a Little Dance/Danger Looming:
After the Midpoint. (S)
- Celebration but danger looming. Protagonist might have temporarily defeated inner or outer demons. May party, make love, be joyous, but it's temporary.
- Doubts begin, either within the team or the protagonist.
- The antagonist is not through yet, not by a long shot.

9. Revelation and/or Obstacle:

New piece of information, new event or new obstacle that pushes the protagonist toward the crisis moment. (M or S)

Options:
- Someone that the protagonist thought was an ally turns out to be an opponent.
- The audience may learn something that the protagonist does not know.
- The protagonist learns something about himself or his history that he did not know.
- The protagonist learns something about the opponent or major conflict in the story that he did not know →
the new information pushes the protagonist to a mini crisis.

──────────── End ACT 2 ────────────

──────────── ACT 3 Begins Here ────────────

10. The Mini Crisis: at 75%

You are now leaving ACT 2. ACT 3 begins here. (M or S)
- This is a major turning point.
- Think: bad news, failure, rising conflict.
- Think: The antagonist is visible or has upped their game. Ending Want is emerging.

11. New Self Emerging:

Can be a moment where the protagonist finally understands how to vanquish the evil beast, how to conquer their inner demons and solve their problems. While the protagonist now has an idea as to how to win the final battle, it is still just an idea, and putting it into action will be challenging. (M or S)

The protagonist takes the lessons and new tools gained along the journey and tries them out. It's difficult, but the new tools enable the protagonist to take on old problems and foes in new ways. The biggest challenge is still ahead, and the protagonist, whether she knows it or not, is in for a big battle. This often leads to deep contemplation.

12. It's Not Looking Good:

The story is heating up and the tension is high. The moment in the ending half of the movie when my dad would always squeeze my hand and say, "Marn, it's not looking good." (S)

- May have experienced the New Self but the problem still exists. Nothing is going our protagonist's way and we have no idea how she might solve the problem.
- The false defeat has sunk in. The protagonist thinks it's a real defeat and that there is no way out.
- Our protagonist faces the biggest choice of their life → be a victim and give up or face their greatest fears to become the protagonist of their own story.
- The last battle with the antagonist, opponent or Old Self is on!
- Good vs. evil may be fighting it out, and evil is strong.
- Protagonist begins to face deepest, darkest fears, and it's tough.
- Protagonist has lost all hope.
- Old Self may have the upper hand.

13. Last Big Decision: Old vs. New Self

Right before the climax/close to the climax. (M or S, usually M)
- This is truly it; the protagonist must make a decision here, either to return to what they know (the Old Self) or to make that last, final transition to → the New Self.

- If it's a happy ending or a comedy, then the Old Self is destroyed and the New Self wins.
- If it's a tragedy, the Old Self is winning.

14. Climax: 95%-98%
Top of the mountain, the height of the conflict. (M or S)
- Good vs. evil forces duke it out here, and only one can win.
- The ultimate confrontation.
- Hold up the tension and the stakes until the peak of the climax, for after the climax the tension of the story is released.
- Usually the place when the New Self wins.

15. The Wrap Up: The Ending
(S or M, usually S)
The final pages, the falling action.
Now we know the protagonist has either chosen to shed his Old Self and embrace the New Self or did not embrace the New Self and has remained the same.
- If the protagonist has chosen the New Self → how has this experience changed the protagonist? What has he learned, how has she grown or become fully realized? How does the protagonist act in his world? How will he make an impact on his world?
- If the protagonist has chosen the Old Self → how has this experience impacted the protagonist, if at all? What has he refused to learn? Will anything change in the protagonist's life, or is she doomed to repeat the same mistakes over and over again?
- What is the new normal for our protagonist?

Frequently Asked Questions About the 15 Plot Spots:

Q: Am I writing the 15 Plot Spots from the protagonist's point of view?

A: Yes. Think about what your protagonist is doing during each plot spot.

Q: What if it is an ensemble cast?

A: Usually there is one person that stands out just a smidge more as the main character (and this helps with the storytelling anyway), so use that person's point of view if at all possible. If not, think of the group as the protagonist. The group as a whole will be traveling through a character arc from an "Old Self" to a "New Self."

Q: What if the last big decision and the climax are the same/occur at the same moment?

A: That's totally normal. The last-big-decision moment can happen anywhere right around the climax moment: before, during or after. Adhere to the logic of your story.

Q: How much time/how many pages should I spend on the wrap-up?

A: Not too much (best suggestion is a few pages). Once we have resolution about the fate of the protagonist, most of the story tension has been released. At that point, we just want a short, clear understanding of how the protagonist is existing in their world.

Q: How do the percentages work?

A: Here's an example. Your here-we-go moment should happen at about one quarter (25 percent) of the way into your piece. So let's say you plan on writing a book that is 300 pages (you can estimate). Your here-we-go moment would be around page 75 (give or take).

Q: Does a plot have to be linear? (Travel through time from young to old?)

A: No, that is entirely up to you. Some stories make sense when they are told in a linear fashion. For others, jumping around in time is what makes the plot exciting.

"A plot isn't merely a string of occurrences; it is a carefully orchestrated telling of events that might include breaking up their temporal order, taking out certain pieces or emphasizing other pieces. It is in that manipulation that a simple story becomes a plot." —Robert Kernen, author of *Building Better Plots*

Q: How many times does a writer do their 15 Plot Spots until they are happy with them?

A: On average, it takes about five attempts until a writer really loves their Plot Spots and feels ready to write scenes.

THREE EXAMPLES OF COMPLETED PLOT SPOTS
from three stories you may know and love → *The Alchemist*; *Eat, Pray, Love*; and *The Lord of the Rings*.

Example #1: 15 Essential Plot Spots for *The Alchemist*, a novel by Paulo Coelho

1. The Grabber: The protagonist, Santiago the shepherd, is excited because he is going to meet the merchant's daughter in four days. She is the girl he met the previous year while traveling, and it was love at first sight. Meeting her made him consider leaving the life of a wanderer and staying in one place. He has been dreaming of her for a year.

2. Old Self in Old World: Santiago is a lonely shepherd who loves to read. He is smart, sensitive and sweet. He reads to his flock and loves to travel. He attended the seminary until he was 16, then he told his father, "I don't want to be a priest, I want to travel." Here's the setup:

- Three days until he meets the merchant's daughter.
- Santiago has been having a recurring dream.
- Goes into a town and gets his dream interpreted by a mystic woman who tells him he needs to go to the pyramids to "get his treasure."
- Turns in an old book he has read for a new one. This book discusses the idea of a "personal legend."
- Meets an old man on a bench in town. The old man says he is the King of Salem, and he will help Santiago find his treasure.
- Santiago doesn't really know himself yet, *and some part of him knows that.*

Personal legend: It's identifying our purpose in life and pursuing it.

3. This Changes Everything/The Catalyst: The King of Salem tells Santiago that he must go to Egypt, get his treasure and follow his personal legend. The King of Salem tells Santiago to follow the omens. Santiago changes his plans. Instead of continuing on to meet the merchant's daughter, he sells his sheep.

4. Struggles and Prep:

Struggles with the Journey: Santiago struggles with the decision to leave his sheep, his shepherd's life and the merchant's daughter—for total uncertainty. Yet he feels compelled to pursue his personal legend.

Prepares for the Journey: The King of Salem tells Santiago to follow the omens to the pyramids to find his treasure. He states, "God has prepared a path for everyone to follow. You just have to read the omens that he left for you."

The King also gives him two stones, Urim and Thummim. Black stone = yes. White stone = no. The stones will help him read the omens. He offers the instructions: "Follow your personal legend through to its conclusion."

The King of Salem shares one last story about finding the secret of happiness: Travel, but never forget your sheep (never forget home).

──────────── End ACT 1 ────────────

──────────── ACT 2 Begins Here ────────────

5. Here We Go: Santiago launches his journey and soon arrives in Tangier.

6. Rough Landing/Small Victories:

<u>Small Victories</u>: In the first bar he enters, Santiago makes a new friend who speaks Spanish. He decides to hire this friend as his guide to get him to the pyramids.

<u>Rough Landing</u>: His new friend/guide says he needs to buy two camels and takes Santiago to a marketplace where he ends up stealing all of Santiago's money.

Obstacle: Santiago meets the crystal merchant and takes a job selling crystal to survive. The crystal merchant tells Santiago he will never be able to make it to Egypt, no matter how long he works.

Revelation: Santiago has an idea to sell tea in the crystal glasses. This move changes the business and they begin to make a lot of money.

Revelation: Santiago yearns to return home, to buy sheep and return to life as he knew it.

Revelation: Santiago realizes he can't go back home; he must go to the pyramids. He joins a caravan.

Obstacles: There are fierce tribal wars throughout the desert. The entire caravan is scared; they must travel in silence and not make fire or call attention to themselves.

7. The Gut: Finding the oasis. Audience meets the Alchemist. Santiago wonders if this is the end of his journey—*maybe this is his treasure?* How do you know when you are at the end of your journey?

8. Do a Little Dance/Danger Looming:

<u>Do a Little Dance</u>: After experiencing the fear of the war and having arrived at the oasis, all members of the caravan are greatly relieved. They laugh and celebrate in delight. The oasis is a safe zone; no war happens there.

Santiago once again experiences love at first sight with a new girl, named Fatima. He wonders if maybe *she* is his treasure.

<u>Danger Looming</u>: Santiago sees a vision while watching hawks in the desert. The vision foretells that war will soon come to haunt the oasis.

9. Revelation and/or Obstacle:

Obstacle: After telling the chiefs of the oasis about his vision, the chiefs tell Santiago, "If you are right, we will give you gold; if you are lying, you will be killed."

Revelation: The Alchemist says he will help Santiago find his treasure. Santiago says goodbye to Fatima though he doesn't want to leave her. He vows to return to her one day. Santiago and the Alchemist set off into the desert toward the pyramids.

Revelation: Deep in the desert, they experience many silent days. This gives Santiago a lot of time to listen and get to know his own heart.

―――――――――――― End ACT 2 ――――――――――――

―――――――――――― ACT 3 Begins Here ――――――――――――

10. The Mini Crisis: The Alchemist and Santiago have entered the war zone. They are taken prisoner by armed men. All of their money is stolen, and they are accused of being spies. To save their lives, the Alchemist tells the men that Santiago can turn himself into the wind in just two days' time.

11. New Self Emerging: Santiago reflects on his silent days in the desert where he came to know his heart and started to believe in his own power. Maybe he *can* turn himself into wind?

12. It's Not Looking Good: Santiago returns to experiencing doubt and, ultimately, does not think he can turn himself into wind. He misses Fatima greatly, doubts his entire journey, and feels he might die. Somehow at the last minute, he can communicate with the soul of the world and, indeed, he turns himself into wind.

Santiago can leave the war zone to finally pursue his treasure at the pyramids. Santiago finally arrives at the pyramids, and he is once again robbed of all his money.

13. Last Big Decision/Old vs. New Self: When Santiago is cruelly robbed and all seems lost, he somehow remains filled with faith.

14. Climax: At the pyramids, Santiago can't find his treasure. The men who robbed him give him information—and with that information he finally realizes where his treasure is at last.

15. The Wrap Up/The Ending: Santiago follows the robbers' information. Santiago finds his own treasure buried under a tree. He then prepares to head back to be with the love of his life, Fatima. Last words: "I'm coming Fatima."

Message: Life is generous to those who pursue their personal legend and never give up.

The Coolest Thing About Noel

There are a lot of cool things about Noel. She writes about a huge fish that looms in fantastical oceans, acting as the antagonist to a woman seeking to find her missing boyfriend and recover the missing part of her memory. Cool stuff. I met Noel in a class I taught at UCSD. She took a look at my Plot Spots handout and immediately raised her hand.

"I don't think this always works," she said, calmly, determined, resolute. Matter of fact. That's how she rolls. I began to engage in my usual banter to lure a student to the dark side of structure. Nothing worked. Finally, I told her maybe she should just try it out.

Well, she took the challenge. She read three books and tested out the Plot Spots against them. She came back the next week.

"Well, I guess it works," she said with a smile. Noel later joined one of my writers' groups, and I saw her amazing skills at all kinds of editing and critiquing along with her writing talent. In fact, often if there is a logic issue—if we are all confused how to fix a plot problem—Noel is the "go-to" gal. The following two examples are by Noel.

Example #2: 15 Essential Plot Spots of *Eat, Pray, Love*, a memoir by Elizabeth Gilbert

1. The Grabber: Sitting in a café in Italy and speaking to a handsome Italian man, Liz Gilbert remembers a moment of despair during the failing of her marriage, when she prayed to God for the first time and God answered.

2. Old Self in Old World: Liz is in the middle of a horrible divorce and a tumultuous new relationship, and she is suffering from depression. She is also discovering a desire to learn Italian and a need for a spiritual teacher. Interviewing a medicine man in Bali, she receives an invitation to become his pupil for a year.

3. This Changes Everything/The Catalyst: Liz begins a year of travel in which she hopes to overcome the trauma of her divorce by traveling to Italy to learn pleasure, India to learn devotion and Indonesia to learn balance.

4. Struggles and Prep: Liz's divorce turns nasty as her husband refuses to sign the divorce papers, but in the end, just as Liz learns that she can petition God for things, the divorce goes through and she can continue with her planned year of travel. She arrives in Rome where she takes great joy in the food, language and beauty as well as in the people she meets. She battles with her depression and finds comfort in writing to God. Her pleasure in Italian food and culture renews her physical and mental health.

——————————— End ACT 1 ———————————

——————————— ACT 2 Begins Here ———————————

5. Here We Go: As Liz learns to be happy, she accepts that her loving-but-stormy relationship with her on-again-off-again post-divorce boyfriend causes her too much misery, and she breaks things off for good. After enjoying her remaining time in Italy with friends and food, Liz continues on to India.

6. Rough Landing/Small Victories:

<u>Rough Landing</u>: Liz begins her spiritual training at an Ashram. With the help of the sharp and irreverent Richard from Texas, she comes to understand that she has control issues and realizes that she needs to let go of past baggage.

<u>Small Victories</u>: Though Liz struggles with her wandering thoughts and unresolved issues, she continues to learn to meditate. Through practice, she can experience a glimmer of inner peace.

7. The Gut: Following the directions of a friend from the Ashram, Liz goes to the roof and has a spiritual meeting with her ex-husband in which she makes peace with him and moves on with her life.

8. Do a Little Dance/Danger Looming: Liz accepts her natural tendency toward gregariousness and combines it with her growing wisdom when she acts as hostess for a series of silent retreats. She finds spiritual fulfillment and bliss in helping visitors as they embark on a difficult spiritual journey. Her stay in the Ashram has changed her, but it will not be until she leaves that she understands exactly how. She understands that she is by nature a border-dweller and she has not yet finished finding her path.

9. Revelation and/or Obstacle: After a brief scare in which the Indonesian medicine man Liz planned to study under fails to remember her, Liz manages to jog his memory and he joyfully takes her on as a pupil. Life is happy and easy for her in Bali as she practices both her Indian yoga and the medicine man's teachings and makes friends with some of the locals, including a struggling, divorced healer named Wayan. Most of the ghosts of Liz's past have ceased to haunt her, but the prompting of friends makes her realize that she should not eschew romantic relationships forever.

End ACT 2

―――――――――――― ACT 3 Begins Here ――――――――――――

10. The Mini Crisis: A night of partying and flirting throws Liz back into crisis, threatening her new identity and the peace she has found.

11. New Self Emerging: The bourgeoning possibility of a relationship with an older Brazilian man leaves Liz fighting for control over herself and she tries to fall back on the simpler pleasures and rigors of her year of eating and praying rather than face the dangers of falling in love again. She begins to face the fact that eating and praying are not enough, and she begins a relationship with Felipe. In her newfound happiness, she is becoming more able to help others, and she raises money to buy a house for her friend, Wayan, who is in dire straits.

12. It's Not Looking Good: Liz's efforts to help Wayan find a house are coming to nothing for reasons Liz doesn't understand. Every property they look at is slightly wrong for subtle reasons, and Liz's time in Bali is running out. The property must be bought before she leaves, and her friend seems unable to decide.

13. Last Big Decision/Old vs. New Self: Liz's relationship with Felipe is growing more serious, and Liz is worried about the logistics of their separate countries and frightened that she is not centered enough to be the center of someone else's world. She realizes at last that she is fighting too hard for control of things that can't be controlled, and she accepts that Felipe is in love with her and that she too is falling in love with him.

14. Climax: Understanding at last that Wayan is lying and deliberately dragging her feet on the property deal, Liz puts her foot down by claiming that the money will disappear if Wayan does not buy property before Liz leaves. Wayan buys the property immediately, and Liz is free to tie up the last loose ends of this stage of her life, embarking on a new life with Felipe.

15. The Wrap Up/The Ending: Liz returns to the Indonesian island of Gil Meno, which she visited two years ago during the messy dissolution of her marriage. She came alone to the island during the darkest and most painful part of that journey, when she promised herself she would remain there until the warring demons in her head were reconciled. It was the first place she found some measure of comfort and peace during that painful time though there was still a long journey ahead of her. Now, she returns there, happy and in love, before she and Felipe embark on an unknown future.

Example #3: 15 Essential Plot Spots of *The Lord of the Rings* by J.R.R. Tolkien

1. The Grabber: The ring that Bilbo found during *The Hobbit* and which he has now given to Frodo is actually the corrupting and terrifyingly powerful One Ring, imbued with the evil power of the Dark Lord Sauron.

2. Old Self in Old World: Frodo lives comfortably at home in the Shire, and though he feels a pull toward the outside world, he does not want to leave home.

3. This Changes Everything/The Catalyst: Black Riders threaten the Shire, searching for Frodo and his Ring. Frodo accepts the quest to take the Ring to Rivendell where the wise elves will know what to do with it. Frodo, Sam, Merry and Pippin set out, though they have barely been outside their village before.

4. Struggles and Prep: The four hobbits are ill-equipped to deal with adventures in the outside world. As the Black Riders hunt them, the hobbits make their way through dangerous magical forests and the haunted Barrow Downs, needing to be rescued twice by the ancient magical being Tom Bombadil. They reach the town of Bree where they naively draw too much attention to themselves. They meet Strider/Aragorn, who will help them reach Rivendell. The Black Riders continue to chase them and eventually stab Frodo with a poisoned knife. It is only with Aragorn's help and the eventual intervention of the elves that they make it to Rivendell alive.

End ACT 1

ACT 2 Begins Here

5. Here We Go: Frodo and his friends recuperate in Rivendell and hope to go home soon. They learn, however, that the Ring cannot stay there and no one else dares to touch it for fear of being corrupted by its power. Frodo accepts the quest to take the Ring to Mordor.

6. Rough Landing/Small Victories: The Fellowship of the Ring sets out and is soon beset by long roads, spies, cold, impassable snowy mountains, and an underground passage in which Gandalf, the leader of the party, dies. Though there are momentary victories, including a rejuvenating stay in Lothlorien, things continue to worsen. Boromir is overcome by the temptation of the Ring and attacks Frodo, who flees, breaking the Fellowship. Boromir dies, and Merry and Pippin are taken by orcs. Aragorn, Legolas, and Gimli, realizing there is nothing more they can do for Frodo and Sam, pursue the orcs.

7. The Gut: Aragorn, Legolas and Gimli discover that Gandalf was not killed but transformed, and he will lead them again.

8. Do a Little Dance/Danger Looming: Gandalf and the remaining fellowship save King Theoden from his poisonously bad advisor and make an alliance with him. Meanwhile, Merry and Pippin enlist the help of the ents. Sauron's forces attack Theoden's people in Helm's Deep and nearly take the fortress, but they are overcome by last-minute help from Gandalf and the ents. The Fellowship and their allies overthrow the evil wizard Saruman.

9. Revelation and/or Obstacle: Frodo and Sam are held back from their quest by impassable roads they have no idea how to navigate. They capture Gollum and convince him to guide them; he is treacherous, but he knows the area and wants to keep the Ring safe. They can move forward now though they fear Gollum will turn on them. Gollum leads them through Shelob's lair, where Shelob, the giant spider, attacks them. Frodo is stung, and Sam, thinking he is dead, is forced to take the Ring. Orcs find Frodo and reveal that he is only stunned by the venom—but he is now in the hands of the ferocious orcs, and Sam must somehow get him back.

Pippin touches a dangerous seeing-stone owned by Saruman, and Gandalf takes him to Gondor, where the steward Denethor is hostile, suspicious, and unhelpful. The vast forces of Mordor gather to attack Gondor, and Gondor has no hope of driving them back on its own. Denethor's son is near death, and Denethor, whose mind is poisoned by another of the seeing stones, goes insane and tries to burn himself and his son before the city is overcome.

End ACT 2

ACT 3 Begins Here

10. The Mini Crisis: Armies led by Theoden and Aragorn arrive just in time and turn the tide of battle. Gondor is saved, for now, but the forces of good are weakened and the forces of Mordor still vastly outnumber them.

11. New Self Emerging: Knowing there is no chance of a military victory against Mordor, Gandalf and Aragorn place all their hopes on Frodo's quest to destroy the Ring. They lead the small and hopelessly outnumbered remainder of their army to attack Mordor in order to distract Sauron's eye away from the hobbits. Sam storms the orcs' tower and rescues Frodo. He returns the Ring. Frodo shows growing signs of the Ring's corrupting influence though he is still managing to fight it.

12. It's Not Looking Good: Exhausted and nearly out of food and water, Frodo and Sam cross Mordor and make their way up Mount Doom. The closer they get, the heavier the Ring grows, until Frodo can only crawl or be carried by Sam. The Ring's power over Frodo is increasing.

13. Last Big Decision/Old vs. New Self: They reach the edge of the molten crater of Mount Doom, and Frodo declares that he will not destroy the Ring after all. He puts it on and vanishes.

14. Climax: Gollum attacks Sam, knocking him out, and then leaps on Frodo. He manages to bite off Frodo's finger and so obtains the Ring again. He dances with joy and falls into the volcano, which destroys the Ring.

15. The Wrap Up/The Ending: Sam drags Frodo from the mouth of the erupting volcano as Sauron's power disintegrates. Frodo is freed from the corruption of the Ring. With Sauron's power destroyed, the forces of good win the war easily. Sam and Frodo are taken from Mount Doom by eagles and healed though Frodo retains lingering effects of his ordeal. Aragorn assumes the throne of Gondor and ushers in an era of peace for Middle Earth. The four hobbits return home to find the Shire under the militant control of a greatly weakened Saruman. With the skills they have learned in their travels, they rally their fellow hobbits and overthrow him. They restore the Shire, and Hobbiton prospers again. Frodo, however, is permanently damaged by his time with the Ring and departs from Middle Earth with Gandalf and the elves.

Want more examples? See Appendix 2 for completed Plot Spots of *Harry Potter and the Sorcerer's Stone*, *Pride and Prejudice* and *Thelma and Louise*.

MAKE PLOTTING YOUR OWN:

There are many ways to bring the outlining and plotting process to life. Find your way. Some examples are creating a note-card board, using plotting software and my personal favorite:

Nancy's Clothesline

Nancy is a wonderful and creative memoirist. When she adopted the Plot Spots, being the teacher that she is, she wanted a way to make them her own—and she wanted it to be visual and tactile.

So, Nancy wrote each of the 15 Plot Spots onto their own individual recipe card. Then she hung up a clothesline. Next she attached each card to the line. This method has caught on and now, in our circle, "Clotheslining It" has sort of become synonymous with plotting.

Often Asked Questions

Q: Okay so I have all my Plot Spots down, do I have to write them in order?

A: Actually NO. Because you can FRANKENSTEIN it.

Say what?

Yep, you can write it *out of order* and then shove it together.

Some writers love to write their stories from beginning to end, one scene organically building upon the next from start to finish. *Some* writers love to do it that way, but not most. Most writers want to write the scenes that call to them, the ones that they feel excited to write. On Monday, they might write the ending. Then on Tuesday, they might write the catalyst, and on Wednesday, they might write the middle. Is this still progress? Yes.

Q: But if I'm writing in pieces and patches, won't it be clunky and awkward?

A: Yes, but most first drafts are just that, clunky and awkward. Your Frankenstein draft will not look pretty. The arm will be stuck awkwardly into the torso and the head may be about to fall off. But your story will still have its basic shape, which is all you need for a first draft.

Once you embrace Frankensteining, it really can be quite fun. You've already thought through your structure, so you can write whatever scene you want to write in whatever order you want to write it. Don't worry about the transition scenes. In the next draft, you can go back and smooth it out, making sure it flows, connects logically and looks pretty.

Okay, your turn. Give it a shot! Remember, it takes a few drafts to whip your plot into shape.

15 Plot Spots Worksheet

1. The Grabber _____
   _____

2. Old Self in Old World _____
   _____

3. This Changes Everything/The Catalyst _____
   _____

4. Struggles and Prep _____
   _____

5. Here We Go _____
   _____

6. Rough Landing/Small Victories _____
   _____

7. The Gut (Middle) _____
   _____

8. Do a Little Dance/Danger Looming _____
   _____

9. Revelation/Obstacle _____
   _____

10. The Mini Crisis _____
    _____

11. New Self Emerging _____
    _____

12. It's Not Looking Good _____
    _____

13. Last Big Decision: Old vs. New Self _____
    _____

14. Climax _____
    _____

15. The Wrap Up _____
    _____

Now, are you ready to learn about pouring?

Okay, there are three rules:

Instructions for Pouring

1. NO THINKING ALLOWED.

2. PUT PEN TO PAPER. IMAGINE TURNING ON THE TAP IN YOUR MIND AND ALLOW THE THOUGHTS TO FLOW FREELY.

3. PUT IT ALL DOWN. (YES, ALL OF IT.)

Optional but recommended: Be joyous and free!

Q: What if pouring doesn't come that easy to me?

A: Good point. It can take time to get in touch with the muse, trust your intuition and feel free enough to let it all out. Here are some ideas.

Pouring Tips

- Keep a small notebook with you at all times.
- Digitally record your thoughts when you get them.
- Go back to Tool #1 (Tenacious WRITING ROUTINE) and remind yourself what time of day and what method works best for you.
- Meditate first.
- Ask your muse to help. "Hey Muse, what you got for me today?"
- Use Prompts. (Just Google *writing prompts:* There are oh, so many.)
- Ask yourself a specific question, then put pen to paper to answer it.
- Take breaks in nature.
- Write in nature.
- Use a brainstorming app to get you started.
- Remind yourself that no one will read what you are writing; these words are just for you.
- In the morning before you write (or get too critical of yourself), set your intention to allow the words to flow out freely and easily.
- Do "Morning Pages" from *The Artist's Way* by Julia Cameron.
- If you start to analyze what you are writing, swiftly bring your attention back to the act of writing words on the page, nothing else.
- Remember that this is not the time to process the thoughts, organize the thoughts or categorize the thoughts. This is the time to capture any and all thoughts.
- Applaud absurdity. If what you are writing doesn't make sense, it's okay. (It may later.)

How some writers have expressed how they POUR it all out:

"I use Wednesday mornings as my pour days. From 10-11 a.m. every week, I allow myself to puke out whatever words are waiting for the page."

"I like to pour every morning, really early, even before coffee—sort of—before I really start thinking even."

"If I'm stuck on a scene, I will go to my pour notebook, it's just a spiral-bound notebook, and I will make myself babble into it for a half a page. Half the time I get really good stuff."

"I have one notebook; the two notebook thing just got too bulky. When I have an idea that is for the plot I just write PLOT at the top of the page, when I want to just get my thoughts out uncensored I write POUR at the top. Every two weeks or so I look it all over and pull out my best stuff."

"I buy a really nice leather-bound journal that is just for me. It's small enough to keep with me, and three times a day I remind myself to take five minutes to pour out my thoughts. It's only 15 minutes a day, but it has made me so much more productive."

"I like to pour during the beginning stages of writing. While I'm still in the outlining phase, I will spend most of my time thinking or pouring, pouring or thinking."

"I go for a walk, and as soon as good stuff starts to come, I pull out my phone and record it."

"I go to a pretentious coffee shop where everyone looks like they are thinking up something brilliant. I write crap while sipping espresso. It's highly satisfying."

What Marni says on pouring: *I firmly believe that if you trusted, you would realize that you know what works for you. Trust yourself. Trust your process.*

(But if you want more ideas to play around with, see Tool #7.)

Takeaway Lessons for Tool #5
PLOT AND POUR

1. The 15 Plot Spots is a plotting tool that the beginning or advanced writer can use.

2. Learning how to plot and pour means you are learning how to look at your story from two very important angles: One using the intuitive-creative lens and the other using the structural and analytical lens.

3. Plotting is when you lay your story idea out, step by step, into a structure.

4. Pouring is when you turn off your thinking/analytical brain and tap into the spirit of the piece. It's when you write with no rules at all.

5. You will plot and pour throughout much of the writing journey. Plot when you can and pour when you need to. If something isn't going right structurally, look back at the plot. If the story is not feeling authentic or alive, do a little pouring.

TOOL #6

Writing the Compelling SCENE with Depth, Originality *and* Special Sauce

"It's none of their business that you have to learn to write. Let them think you were born that way."
—Ernest Hemingway

What You Have Done So Far

Tool #1: By figuring out where you write best, how you write best and by creating a nurturing place to write, you have given yourself the best chance at writing success.

Tool #2: By working to craft a solid story idea and theme, you have laid a strong foundation upon which to build your story.

Tool #3: By traveling through the 9 Character Elements, you have added compelling characters to your creative stew.

Tool #4: By learning the 3 Key Spots, you have given your story a basic shape.

Tool #5: By learning how to navigate the major story beats in a plot while still allowing for spontaneous creativity, you are armed to craft a kick-ass plot.

Just look how far you've come! You've done a lot of macro (big picture) work. Now it's time to do a little micro (little picture) work. You want the journey to be fun, right? That means you want each scene to be both *compelling* and *vibrant*. So now the time has come to dive in and see how you can bring all those smaller moments to life. (It's not that hard. I've got your back.)

Q: What is a scene?

A: It's one building block of your story. Think of your story as a long railroad track. Each plank in the track is a scene. One must lead to the next, which leads to the next…

Checklist for Effective Scene Writing

Think

- **GROUNDING**
- **CONFLICT**
- **PURPOSE/FORWARD MOTION**
- **SHOWING**
- **SHAPE**

Late one night in a read and critique group not too far from your very town, this terribly awkward scene went down:

(*Picture a room in the back of a hip coffee house and eight fidgety, over-caffeinated writers sitting in a circle, all confused.*)

7 ESSENTIAL WRITING TOOLS

Girl: I just don't understand what's going on in this scene.

Boy: He's an alien. She's like a robot-cyborg. They're talking.

Girl: But how do we know he's an alien? How do we know she's a cyborg?

Boy: It should be obvious by the way they're talking.

Girl: But where are they? And why is this scene even in the book?

Boy: I'm not entirely sure, but this was the dialogue that came to me when I first thought about writing this book. Besides, I spent two weeks writing it and it's my turn to read, so we are reading it.

Girl: But they're just talking in nonsensical outbursts. And we don't know where they are, and like, nothing happens. They just sit there the whole time.

Boy: Didn't you understand the subtext? The metaphors? The layered innuendos?

Girl: No.

Group Leader (Me): Could anyone follow the scene?

Slowly, sadly all of the writers shook their heads no. The author was furious.

My mind raced. I was in a mad-dash panic as I tried to figure out how to somehow turn this crash-and-burn moment into a positive, teachable moment. But the truth was: It was possibly the very worst scene I had ever read. Ever.

The next week at group, we began discussing the elements that are necessary to construct a good scene. People brought in scenes from films, books, plays and memoirs. They brought in the scenes that everyone remembered. (You know: The ones that have made us laugh, cry, cringe or curse out loud.) I repeated this exercise for the next three years with different groups. And always, when it came right down to it, the best scenes had the following five qualities:

Grounding → Conflict → Purpose → Showing → Shape

Let's break it down:

GROUNDING

<u>In a Nutshell</u>: Where are we, and who is there?
More specifically
→ Whose eyes are we looking through? What is the point of view?
→ Where are we physically? Outside or inside? What does it look like?
→ What other characters are there?
→ What is the year? The time? The date?
→ Any other information we need? Is it raining, snowing, a holiday or a special event?

Grounding is HUGE. Huge, huge, huge.

It sounds obvious, but I have found that many writers forget to simply tell their reader where they are, who is there and what everyone looks like.

You can eliminate a ton of confusion by simply offering the reader a little bit of basic information.

DISCLAIMERS and QUALIFIERS

Q: Wait a second: Won't that get repetitive? Do I have to use grounding in every scene?

A: No way, José! Meaning NO, you absolutely do not have to use grounding in every scene. If you have already grounded your readers in the last scene as to where they are and who is with them, your readers will be happy.

Q: When do you need new grounding?

A: When you switch locations, time periods, points of view or when you add or subtract characters to the scene.

Q: What if I want to be purposefully confusing, like say in a dream sequence?

A: As long as it's on purpose, have at it. Just don't keep us confused for too long.

CONFLICT

Conflict is
→ The substance of writing. It's the juicy stuff, it's the heart of the matter, and it's the meat. When conflict is presented well, there's just the right amount of dramatic tension.

Q: Hey, what's the right amount of dramatic tension?

A: Just enough to keep the reader interested, to wonder and to care what will happen next.

Remember to
- Play with suspense.
- Remind us of the stakes.
- Use internal conflict (inner dialogue can often do the trick).
- End on conflict (especially at the end of a chapter).
- Use subtext when appropriate.

DISCLAIMERS and QUALIFIERS

Q: Do I want conflict in every scene? Won't the reader get fatigued?

A: While you don't want to let your protagonist out of danger until the very end, you will most likely vary the levels of conflict. Some scenes may be purposefully slow or comedic to allow the reader a moment to breathe while other scenes may be crafted with high tension to keep readers on their toes. But even in low-conflict scenes, the tension is still there—unsolved and unresolved until the end.

PURPOSE/FORWARD MOTION

Every scene should serve a purpose and in some way move the story forward. The essential (needed) scenes will reveal or foreshadow information and/or reveal elements of character.

In understanding the purpose of a scene, ask yourself: DO YOU, the author, know why the scene is there?

Writing Tip: We are not talking about knowing the point of your whole story, or the point of life or the point of a pencil. Just why you think <u>this scene</u> belongs in <u>this story</u>.

Ask

- How does this scene move the story forward or reveal character information?
- Is this scene a repeat of old information?
- Does this scene move us closer to the climax?

Quick and Easy Keep-or-Cut Tool

If you're ever wondering if you should keep or cut a scene, ask the following questions:

→ Does this scene push the story forward or reveal character? If so, how?
→ Have I already communicated this story information and/or character information? Is it a repeat?
→ Do we need this scene as a breather scene (a moment to rest, reflect or add humor to an intense section)?

Important note: Sometimes authors are too close to their work and can't tell if they're repeating information. If you find yourself in this category, get yourself some trusted, experienced readers or editors.

DISCLAIMERS and QUALIFIERS

There are times you'll want to repeat information, especially if you want to reinforce an idea or concept. In this case, repetition is still forward motion.

SHOWING

Am I **showing** instead of **telling**?

Telling is: a list or a catalog of events, actions and/or emotions.

Showing is: Creating an image in the reader's mind. It's bringing the moment to life for the reader so they feel as if they're IN the experience.

In essence: Help the reader to feel the emotions you are trying to convey.

Remember the shirt the agent had on at that conference? → "Make Me Care." It's the same thing here. Make your reader care.

Example: This author is writing a story about a man who is coming to terms with the fact that his wife has died.

WRONG: *I'll never forget how I felt when I looked at our bedroom. I was angry and sad. My heart was broken, and I thought I'd never get over that lonely feeling. And also, I had no one to share good news with.*

This only provides the reader with a list of events and emotions. The reader in no way feels what the writer feels. Reader doesn't care.

EH… AVERAGE: *I didn't know if I'd ever get over Susan's death. I felt like curling into a ball and crying every time I had good news but couldn't tell her. She was the only one I wanted to tell. She had the best smile; she loved art and she might have been the only person who cared what happened to me.*

There are some more details and description, but they don't help us to care about the author or the person they are writing about. These details help the writing to be less dry, but it is still telling. The reader sort of cares.

BETTER: *Three weeks ago I got a raise. I hadn't gotten a raise in six and a half years. I grabbed my coat and jumped in the car to speed home. This meant I could finally take Susan on that trip to New Mexico to see the*

Ixtapa Gallery she'd always wanted to see. I ran two red lights. I loved telling her good news. Her nose would crinkle and her eyes would light up. I swear that woman could dance on good news for a week. I ran upstairs and opened the bedroom door, and then I remembered. I choked on the emptiness of the stark white bedroom.

Here the author has painted a scene that shows us how much he loves his wife, that she is the center of his world—making it a painful moment to realize that she is really gone. The reader cares.

Series of Questions on Showing

1. Think of using the senses: How did things look, feel, taste, smell and sound? Any colors or music?
2. Would dialogue help to bring this moment alive?
3. What was the weather like?
4. Are any symbols used? Is there an image that represents a larger idea in the book?
5. What emotions did your characters experience in the moment? How did they behave? How did others behave? What was the overriding emotion of the moment?
6. Am I paying attention to subtext?
    a. Subtext is the underlying or implicit meaning when the reader can infer the meaning though the writer hasn't stated it directly. Hemingway called it, the "Iceberg Theory." He said that only one-eighth of the iceberg is visible. Subtext is when we're not discussing the full iceberg, even though we all know it's there. Some say it's the art of omission.
7. Am I utilizing contrast?
    a. Contrast is taking two differing ideas and creating a new and unique combination.

b. Contrast is placing two opposing items next to one another to highlight their differences.

Q: Hey, where might I find places to inject contrast?

A: Look in these areas

- Contrast within your characters
- Contrast between characters
- Contrast within scenes
- Contrast between scenes
- Contrast with situations
- Contrast with setting/weather

Utilizing contrast is such a simple idea, but writers forget to use it.

DISCLAIMERS and QUALIFIERS

Q: Do I always need to SHOW everything? Isn't there a time to just tell some information?

A: Absolutely. You have to pick and choose. Much information will be told. Often, the most **remembered** information will be shown.

SHAPE

Each scene needs to have a shape. Essentially, each scene has a beginning, middle and end. The scene begins when your character sets out with a short-term goal. The middle of the scene occurs when the character runs into an obstacle. The end of the scene occurs when the character experiences either failure, success or a complication.

The 3 Types of SCENE SHAPE and When They Are Used:

1. Small Goal → Obstacle → Failure (most of the time)

OR

2. Small Goal → Obstacle → Complication (some of the time)

OR

3. Small Goal → Obstacle → Success (some of the time)

Remember: The reason that most of your scenes will end in failure is because you don't want the reader to feel total satisfaction until the end. Keep 'em guessing, wondering, wanting, yearning, hoping, thinking—and, most of all, turning the pages.

BIG goals Little goals It's all about the goals!

In the beginning, your protagonist has a big goal. (Usually your protagonist gets clear and active about their big goal at about the 25 percent mark.)

In other words, your protagonist wants something big and specific. This is your protagonist's overall or long-term goal. The big goal defines the shape of your story.

Example: A girl, let's call her Kate, is trying to get to her boyfriend, Ed, at The Old Spaghetti Factory across town in a huge winter storm. (She thinks he may propose!)

BIG GOAL: Get to The Old Spaghetti Factory Restaurant

But a story about a girl who gets in her car and drives to a restaurant is not a very interesting story. The scenes are what give us the up-and-down journey. The scenes are where our protagonist's character is revealed. The scenes are where we laugh, cry or both.

Thus, we need some scenes in between setting the goal and achieving (or not achieving) the goal.

In each scene, the protagonist faces smaller, short-term goals. The small goals define the shape of your scene.

Most of these goals your protagonist will fail at, to increase the tension and raise the stakes. Some of these goals will be met with complications that increase the tension or humor, and some of the goals will be met successfully so the plot can move forward.

Wondering if and how Kate gets to The Old Spaghetti Factory? Let's look at this series of scenes to illustrate the idea of failure, complication and success:

- Kate gets all dolled up, then gets in her car and it won't turn over (failure).
- Kate gets out of her car with nowhere to turn and then sees that the public bus is running (success).
- Kate hops on the bus and happens to run smack into Mike, an old boyfriend, who makes her laugh (complication).
- As soon as the bus gets on the freeway, it runs into a seriously dangerous ice patch. The road is not drivable (failure).
- All the passengers must get out (complication).
- On the side of the icy road, Kate calls her best friend, Shiloh, who agrees to take her to The Old Spaghetti Factory (success).

- When Shiloh arrives, we find out that she's hosting a wild bachelorette party with her six sisters. Now Kate and her old boyfriend must squeeze into an over-packed limo with six crazy sisters and a wild-woman driver, Gloria (complication).

(And on and on.)

Q: Must my protagonist achieve his or her big goal at the end?

A: No. That's your storytelling decision, as is the ending. Comedy or tragedy, it's up to you.

For example, the story could end where

- Kate makes it to The Old Spaghetti Factory just in time and gets happily, blissfully engaged,
or
- Kate falls in love with Mike, the old boyfriend she met on the bus,
or
- Kate finally arrives at the restaurant but decides not to go in,
or
- Kate makes it to The Old Spaghetti Factory and rushes in to find out her boyfriend, Ed, was trying to break up with her.

It's all up to you.

So, in essence, each scene until the climax

→ Will in some way move the story forward and keep the tension rising, (thus making the reader want to turn the page!).

DISCLAIMERS and QUALIFIERS

Some of your scenes may be clipped short on purpose while others may run long on purpose. A scene can be a paragraph or two to five pages. This is a general guide. Once you get a feeling for the scenes in your story, trust your gut.

EXAMPLES

Let's look at some classic pieces of writing and see what we can uncover. Remember to be on the lookout for

Grounding → Conflict → Purpose → Showing → Shape

Example #1

Metamorphosis by Franz Kafka, Opening Scene

(Who doesn't like a story where a guy goes to bed a traveling salesman and wakes up a bug?)

One morning, when Gregor Samsa woke from troubled dreams, he found himself transformed in his bed into a horrible vermin. He lay on his armor-like back, and if he lifted his head a little he could see his brown belly, slightly domed and divided by arches into stiff sections. The bedding was hardly able to cover it and seemed ready to slide off any moment. His many legs, pitifully thin compared with the size of the rest of him, waved about helplessly as he looked.

"What's happened to me?" he thought. It wasn't a dream. His room, a proper human room although a little too small, lay peacefully between its four familiar walls. A collection of textile samples lay spread out on the table—Samsa was a travelling salesman—and above it there hung a picture that he had recently cut out of an illustrated magazine and housed in a nice, gilded frame. It showed a lady fitted out with a fur hat and fur boa who sat upright, raising a heavy fur muff that covered the whole of her lower arm towards the viewer.

Gregor then turned to look out the window at the dull weather. Drops of rain could be heard hitting the pane, which made him feel quite sad. "How about if I sleep a little bit longer and forget all this nonsense," he thought, but that was something he was unable to do because he was used to sleeping on his right, and in his present state couldn't get into that position. However hard he threw himself onto his right, he always rolled back to where he was. He must have tried it a hundred times, shut his eyes so that he wouldn't have to look at the floundering legs, and only stopped when he began to feel a mild, dull pain there that he had never felt before.

"Oh, God," he thought, "what a strenuous career it is that I've chosen! Travelling day in and day out. Doing business like this takes much more effort than doing your own business at home, and on top of that there's the curse of travelling, worries about making train connections, bad and irregular food, contact with different people all the time so that you can never get to know anyone or become friendly with them. It can all go to Hell!" He felt a slight itch up on his belly; pushed himself slowly up on his back towards the headboard so that he could lift his head better; found where the itch was, and saw that it was covered with lots of little white spots which he didn't know what to make of; and when he tried to feel the place with one of his legs he drew it quickly back because as soon as he touched it he was overcome by a cold shudder.

He slid back into his former position. "Getting up early all the time," he thought, "it makes you stupid. You've got to get enough sleep. Other travelling salesmen live a life of luxury. For instance, whenever I go back to the guest house during the morning to copy out the contract, these gentlemen are always still sitting there eating their breakfasts. I ought to just try that with my boss; I'd get kicked out on the spot. But who knows, maybe that would be the best thing for me. If I didn't have my parents to think about I'd have given in my notice a long time ago, I'd have gone up to the boss and told him just what I think, tell him everything I would, let him know just what I feel. He'd fall right off his desk! And it's a funny sort of business to be sitting up there at your desk, talking down at your subordinates from up there, especially when you have to go right up close because the boss is hard of hearing. Well, there's still some hope; once I've got the money together to pay off my parents' debt to him—another five or six years I suppose—that's definitely what I'll do. That's when I'll make the big change. First of all though, I've got to get up, my train leaves at five."

And he looked over at the alarm clock, ticking on the chest of drawers. "God in Heaven!" he thought. It was half past six and the hands were quietly moving forwards, it was even later than half past, more like quarter to seven. Had the alarm clock not rung? He could see from the bed that it had been set for four o'clock, as it should have been; it certainly must have rung. Yes, but was it possible to quietly sleep through that furniture-rattling noise? True, he had not slept peacefully, but probably all the more deeply because of that. What should he do now? The next train went at seven; if he were to catch that he would have to rush like mad and the collection of samples was still not packed, and he did not at all feel particularly fresh and lively. And even if he did catch the train he would not avoid his boss's anger as the office assistant would have been there to see the five o'clock train go, he would have put in his report about Gregor's not being there a long time ago. The office assistant was the boss's man, spineless, and with no understanding. What about if he reported sick? But that would be extremely strained and suspicious as in fifteen years of service Gregor had never once yet been ill. His boss would certainly come round with the doctor from the medical insurance company, accuse his parents of having a lazy son, and accept the doctor's recommendation not to make any claim as the doctor believed that no-one was ever ill but that many were workshy. And what's more, would he have been entirely wrong in this case? Gregor did in fact, apart from excessive sleepiness after sleeping for so long, feel completely well and even felt much hungrier than usual.

He was still hurriedly thinking all this through, unable to decide to get out of the bed, when the clock struck quarter to seven. There was a cautious knock at the door near his head. "Gregor," somebody called —it was his mother—"it's quarter to seven. Didn't you want to go somewhere?"

—End of Scene—

QUICK SCENE ANALYSIS

Grounding: Gregor is home in his bed (somewhere in the early 1900s).

Conflict: He wakes up, and instead of looking like a human being, he is some sort of large beetle. Stakes: He's a traveling salesman who must get to work, and he is late. *(And did I mention that he's a bug?)*

Purpose/Forward Motion: He's living with his family who will start worrying if he doesn't emerge from the room soon, as he's due on his train at five. The scene introduces the main conflict of the story: The normal everyday life of a man is over as he realizes he's no longer human.

The scene reveals that he's a rational, thoughtful man who lives a fairly in-the-box life with a regimented schedule.

Showing
- Weather: rain, creating a dreary backdrop for the tale.
- Overriding emotion: frustration.
- Senses: how his new body feels, unable to move the way humans do, hungry.
- Contrast: having the physical experience of a bug but the internal consciousness of an overworked traveling salesman late for work.

Shape
1. Long-term goal: Get to the train.
2. Short-term goal: Must get out of bed. The life of a traveling salesman can't wait.
3. Obstacle: Tries to get out of bed, but it's difficult due to having so many vermin legs and an oddly shaped bug body.
4. Failure: The short-term goal was not met. He was unable to get out of bed, and now his mother is calling for him. The stakes have been raised.

Example #2

The Secret Garden by Frances Hodgson Burnett, Chapter 6

In all her wanderings through the long corridors and the empty rooms, she had seen nothing alive; but in this room she saw something. Just after she had closed the cabinet door she heard a tiny rustling sound. It made her jump and look around at the sofa by the fireplace, from which it seemed to come. In the corner of the sofa there was a cushion, and in the velvet which covered it there was a hole, and out of the hole peeped a tiny head with a pair of frightened eyes in it.

Mary crept softly across the room to look. The bright eyes belonged to a little gray mouse, and the mouse had eaten a hole into the cushion and made a comfortable nest there. Six baby mice were cuddled up asleep near her. If there was no one else alive in the hundred rooms there were seven mice who did not look lonely at all.

"If they wouldn't be so frightened I would take them back with me," said Mary.

She had wandered about long enough to feel too tired to wander any farther, and she turned back. Two or three times she lost her way by turning down the wrong corridor and was obliged to ramble up and down until she found the right one; but at last she reached her own floor again, though she was some distance from her own room and did not know exactly where she was.

"I believe I have taken a wrong turning again," she said, standing still at what seemed the end of a short passage with tapestry on the wall. "I don't know which way to go. How still everything is!"

It was while she was standing here and just after she had said this that the stillness was broken by a sound. It was another cry, but not quite like the one she had heard last night; it was only a short one, a fretful, childish whine muffled by passing through walls.

"It's nearer than it was," said Mary, her heart beating rather faster. "And it *is* crying."

She put her hand accidentally upon the tapestry near her, and then sprang back, feeling quite startled. The tapestry was the covering of a door which fell open and showed her that there was another part of the corridor behind it, and Mrs. Medlock was coming up it with her bunch of keys in her hand and a very cross look on her face.

"What are you doing here?" she said, and she took Mary by the arm and pulled her away. "What did I tell you?"

"I turned round the wrong corner," explained Mary. "I didn't know which way to go and I heard some one crying."

She quite hated Mrs. Medlock at the moment, but she hated her more the next.

"You didn't hear anything of the sort," said the housekeeper. "You come along back to your own nursery or I'll box your ears."

And she took her by the arm and half pushed, half pulled her up one passage and down another until she pushed her in at the door of her own room.

"Now," she said, "you stay where you're told to stay or you'll find yourself locked up. The master had better get you a governess, same as he said he would. You're one that needs some one to look sharp after you. I've got enough to do."

She went out of the room and slammed the door after her, and Mary went and sat on the hearthrug, pale with rage. She did not cry, but ground her teeth.

"There *was* some one crying—there *was*—there *was*!" she said to herself.

She had heard it twice now, and sometime she would find out. She had found out a great deal this morning. She felt as if she had been on a long journey, and at any rate she had had something to amuse her all the time, and she had played with the ivory elephants and had seen the gray mouse and its babies in their nest in the velvet cushion.

—End of Scene—

QUICK SCENE ANALYSIS

Grounding: Mary is a young girl in a huge, mysterious and lonely house. She seems troubled and alone—possibly unloved. She has been told not to wander.

Conflict: Mary hears what she believes to be sounds of crying. She sneaks out secretly to find the source of the crying noises.

Purpose/Forward Motion: Mary is not going to do as she is told; she is going to search room to room until she uncovers the house's secrets. This scene reveals information about her character. She is determined and feisty in her desire to explore. The scene also reveals information about the disconnected, uncaring people she lives with. Finally, the scene reveals much about the setting of the novel. The author describes hundreds of still, empty rooms, evoking the image of a large and lonely home. There are secrets to be uncovered if only she looks hard enough.

Showing
- Overriding emotions: anticipation, fear.
- Symbolism: Symbolic image of Mrs. Medlock coming toward her with a hefty bunch of keys. She is a lonely girl. She doesn't talk about her loneliness, yet comments on how unlonely the seven mice are and wishes she could take them back with her. She is obviously in need of company and has a strong desire to connect to something that is alive.
- Contrast: total stillness/silence with the faraway human cry.

Shape
1. Long-term goal: Find the Secret Garden.
2. Short-term goal: to uncover the mystery. What is out there beyond the confines of where she is allowed to go?
3. Obstacle: Hears sounds (human voice crying?) but finds no one.
4. Failure: Her goal is not met. The maid finds her, drags her back and does not believe her.

Example #3

The Wizard of Oz by L. Frank Baum

"How far is it to the Emerald City?" the girl asked.

"I do not know," answered Boq gravely, "for I have never been there. It is better for people to keep away from Oz, unless they have business with him. But it is a long way to the Emerald City, and it will take you many days. The country here is rich and pleasant, but you must pass through rough and dangerous places before you reach the end of your journey."

This worried Dorothy a little, but she knew that only the Great Oz could help her get to Kansas again, so she bravely resolved not to turn back.

She bade her friends goodbye, and again started along the road of yellow brick. When she had gone several miles she thought she would stop to rest, and so climbed to the top of the fence beside the road and sat down. There was a great cornfield beyond the fence, and not far away she saw a Scarecrow, placed high on a pole to keep the birds from the ripe corn.

Dorothy leaned her chin upon her hand and gazed thoughtfully at the Scarecrow. Its head was a small sack stuffed with straw, with eyes, nose, and mouth painted on it to represent a face. An old, pointed blue hat, that had belonged to some Munchkin, was perched on his head, and the rest of the figure was a blue suit of clothes, worn and faded, which had also been stuffed with straw. On the feet were some old boots with blue tops, such as every man wore in this country, and the figure was raised above the stalks of corn by means of the pole stuck up its back.

While Dorothy was looking earnestly into the queer, painted face of the Scarecrow, she was surprised to see one of the eyes slowly wink at her. She thought she must have been mistaken at first, for none of the scarecrows in Kansas ever wink; but presently the figure nodded its head to her in a friendly way. Then she climbed down from the fence and walked up to it, while Toto ran around the pole and barked.

"Good day," said the Scarecrow, in a rather husky voice.

"Did you speak?" asked the girl, in wonder.

"Certainly," answered the Scarecrow. "How do you do?"

"I'm pretty well, thank you," replied Dorothy politely. "How do you do?"

"I'm not feeling well," said the Scarecrow, with a smile, "for it is very tedious being perched up here night and day to scare away crows."

"Can't you get down?" asked Dorothy.

"No, for this pole is stuck up my back. If you will please take away the pole I shall be greatly obliged to you."

Dorothy reached up both arms and lifted the figure off the pole, for, being stuffed with straw, it was quite light.

"Thank you very much," said the Scarecrow, when he had been set down on the ground. "I feel like a new man."

Dorothy was puzzled at this, for it sounded queer to hear a stuffed man speak, and to see him bow and walk along beside her.

"Who are you?" asked the Scarecrow when he had stretched himself and yawned. "And where are you going?"

"My name is Dorothy," said the girl, "and I am going to the Emerald City, to ask the Great Oz to send me back to Kansas."

"Where is the Emerald City?" he inquired. "And who is Oz?"

"Why, don't you know?" she returned, in surprise.

"No, indeed. I don't know anything. You see, I am stuffed, so I have no brains at all," he answered sadly.

"Oh," said Dorothy, "I'm awfully sorry for you."

"Do you think," he asked, "if I go to the Emerald City with you, that Oz would give me some brains?"

"I cannot tell," she returned, "but you may come with me, if you like. If Oz will not give you any brains you will be no worse off than you are now."

—End of Scene—

QUICK SCENE ANALYSIS

Grounding: Dorothy is with her dog, Toto, looking for the Yellow Brick Road. Her goal is to get to the Emerald City in hopes that the Wizard can help her get home.

Conflict: She was told it will be a long and dangerous journey, and it's clear she doesn't know the way.

Purpose/Forward Motion: She heads off alone with her dog and meets her first traveling companion, the Scarecrow. The way she welcomes him along the journey reveals her character: She is a warm, nurturing girl who cares for all. This scene also reveals that she is in for a journey that will be filled with surprises and magical happenings. She's got to really want to get home to get home.

Showing
- Dialogue: This is a dialogue-heavy scene.
- Overriding emotions: anticipation/wonder.
- Contrast: In her normal world, a Scarecrow would not speak. Here in this world, almost anything seems possible.

Shape
1. Long-term goal: Get home to Kansas.
2. Short-term goal: Get to the Emerald City.
3. Obstacle: It's a long journey. She gets tired and stops to rest.
4. Complication: Her goal is not met yet, but she meets a Scarecrow who speaks and wants a brain. He will join her.

So there you go:
Grounding → Conflict → Purpose → Showing → Shape!

Q: But wait! I think I get how to write a scene, but like isn't there something that goes in between scenes?

A: So glad you asked. Remember, I promised special sauce. Well, here it is.

In between scenes, you will find

Sequels!

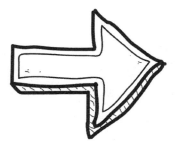

Your character has just experienced a failure, a complication or a small success. Most likely your character will deal with what just occurred and decide what to do next. Why do I call it the "special sauce?" Because knowing how to use a sequel often gives your writing a dash of needed flavor.

Sequels are small and mighty but packed with good things:

- Emotions
- Reactions
- Revelations/Insights
- Planning
- Retreating
- New Goal Making

Since I love to simplify and make things shorter, all those bullet points up there can be reduced to:

Sequels = F → O → N
Feel → Options → New Goal

What does my character **feel** about what just happened?
What are my characters' possible **options**/responses to what just happened?
What is my character's **new goal**?

It might be helpful to look at the sequels of the three scenes we just analyzed.

Metamorphosis
Quick recap of scene: Gregor woke up a large bug. He's a traveling salesman trying to get to work but can't get out of bed.

Sequel
Feel: Gregor feels confused. He also feels frustration that he can't perform a simple task like getting out of bed. How the character responds in the sequel shows who he is. That Gregor Samsa responds to being turned into a cockroach by worrying he'll be late for work says a LOT about Gregor Samsa.
Options: Stay in bed and hide or keep trying to get out of bed.
New Goal: Find another way to get out of bed.

Secret Garden
Quick recap of scene: Mary is a young girl, lonely and alone in a huge house. She hears mysterious cries and looks for the source only to be dragged back and scolded by her caretaker.

Sequel
Feel: Mary feels angered that she heard the cry, that her plans were thwarted and that the only adult in her realm doesn't seem to care or believe her. She also feels both curious and lonely.
Options: She could listen to her caretaker and not venture out again, or she could sneak out later.
New Goal: Find the source of the crying. She will sneak out later.

7 ESSENTIAL WRITING TOOLS

Wizard of Oz
Quick recap of scene: Dorothy discovers she has a long way to go to get to the Emerald City. She stops on the road to rest where she meets a talking scarecrow.

Sequel
Feel: Dorothy feels perplexed and maybe excited by the magic of the people she is encountering; she is also happy to have another traveling companion.
Options: She can continue on the road herself or take the Scarecrow with her.
New Goal: She decides to get back on the Yellow Brick Road with the Scarecrow and find the Wizard together.

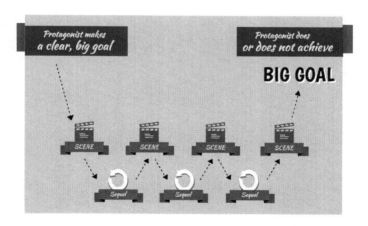

Random critic: UGH, this is so formulaic and boring. If I had to sit down and do this for every scene, I'd puke.

Marni: Yeah. You don't have to. For some, that much analyzing is no fun.

Random critic: That's it? That's all you gotta say?

Marni: Well, to expand, I guess I'd say it's good for every writer to really dive in and take apart this concept until you understand it—at least once. Breaking something down can help you really "get" a concept. You will find that some elements of craft will come to you naturally. But if you struggle with any aspect, then look at it more deeply. I only really studied something and got better when I needed help.

We are almost done, but no understanding of crafting the scene can be complete without touching on dialogue.

Just a Smidge About Dialogue

What's the difference between good and bad dialogue?

Good dialogue
1. Reveals something fun or interesting about the character.
2. Reveals unknown aspects of the relationships between the characters.
3. Moves the plot forward or in some way conveys important information.
4. Prepares an audience for events to come.
5. Provides a needed moment of rest, clarity or humor.
6. Keeps you laughing or crying.
7. Is so juicy you can't believe you just heard it.
8. Is often in fun and interesting settings. (I once had a teacher that for a whole semester would not let us place characters in a diner or a kitchen—forcing us to place the characters in unconventional settings.)

Hint: If dialogue is flat or uninteresting, check to see if it's accomplishing at least two of these goals.

Bad Dialogue

Bad dialogue can come in many packages. But these are the worst offenders.

Watch out for dialogue that is
1. Wordy McWordy: Too long or verbose/using too many words to get your point across.
2. Repeat! Repeat! Repeat!: Too repetitious, repeating the same idea or message over and over.
3. Same! Same! Same!: When several characters sound too much alike so that it is hard to distinguish between the voices.
4. Soap Opera-ish: When the characters constantly speak their real thoughts to the audience.
5. Speechy-Preachy: When dialogue is long-winded or overflowing with the writer's advice to the world.
6. Lecture-ific: Too complete, all thoughts are expressed from start to finish.
7. So On-the-Nose: When dialogue tells instead of suggests.

EXTRA CREDIT!

Marni's Secrets About Getting to the Juice of a Scene

How to fly to the best of your scene and cut the rest.

The rules of a good scene are often the same as going to a party that you think will be fun but turns out to be a dud: Come a little late and leave a little early.

1. **Target the heat of the conflict.** Ask, what is this scene really about? Boil it down to one or two sentences.

    Examples
    - This scene is about the fact that Jocelyn is no longer in love with Dan.
    - This scene is about two men who both want to run a top company their own way, now realizing that only one can be the leader.
    - This scene is about a president realizing that his country is about to go to war.
    - This scene is about two people who have been in love from afar for six years finally admitting they want to kiss.

2. **How to start your juicy scene:** Start your scene in one of two dynamic places or "hot spots."

    Begin
    (A) When the flame is turned on or
    (B) When the oil sizzles

- **When the flame is turned on**: Find the moment when the tension is palpable, when the two opposing forces are finally in the same room, when the elephant in the room is brought up, when the issue is exposed.
- **When the oil sizzles**: This moment is *almost* smack in the middle of the conflict, just before fists fly. This is the moment when, as an audience, you are on the edge of your seat. It is the moment before the emotional peak.

3. **How to end?**

- End on a question. (You can answer it, or begin to answer it, in the next scene.)
- End with an unanswered issue on the table (a cliffhanger).
- End with a shock or a twist—an unexpected (but planted) moment.

Exercise: Pick a scene from the examples above. Try starting at one of the hot spots. Read it out loud to yourself or a group. See if you can start any later in the scene and still have it make sense. See if you can end on a question or a cliffhanger.

Raising the Stakes and Dialogue

These are the kinds of scenes that, by their nature, will help you to attain realistic yet multi-layered dialogue. When appropriate, try to turn up the heat by raising the stakes. I've put a star (*) at the moment that the stakes are raised.

1. **"It's happening but I'm not acknowledging it" kind of scene**

In real life, people often try to avoid problems. Some great scenes involve one person attempting to deal with an issue while another person does everything in his/her power to *not* talk about it. Usually, the tension grows until the "avoider" must speak. Sometimes at that point there is an explosion or all-out confrontation.

Examples

- Lawrence, a guilty husband, has come home to finally confess that he is having an affair, but the wife, Lynn, will only discuss the chicken she is preparing for dinner. *Natalie, his mistress, is waiting in the car.

- Barb, an employee sitting at her cubicle, is about to get fired for having personal conversations during work. She keeps working frantically on a report while the boss is trying to talk to her. *Barb's loud, obnoxious boyfriend is still on speakerphone, and she can't shut it off.

2. **"I'm saying one thing and doing another" kind of scene**

What makes people so much fun to write about is that often, they don't walk their talk. They talk about who they are in the world, yet their behavior is often very different. Capturing that dichotomy can produce insightful (and often funny) dialogue.

Examples

- A man proposes and professes his love while yawning. *This moment is captured on TV and is replayed over and over on local television news channels.

- Two people are deciding to break up because they never want to see one another again as they peel off their clothes and make love. *One has a plane to catch in 30 minutes.

3. **"Two intense wants are in the room" kind of scene**

This is when two people are staring each other down, and they both want the same thing, but only one can have it. If you know the characters (or personality types), it is great fun to put them in a room and watch the sparks fly.

Examples

- Two military commanders want to handle a battle differently. One wants to use chemical warfare and the other wants to try negotiation first. *A decision must be made in 10 minutes or less.

- Two men are vying for the same woman they have both wanted since college. *This is the day before she leaves the country.

4. **"Chemistry, Chemistry, Chemistry" kind of scene**

This is the best kind of scene to write if you are writing a love story. Often, great chemistry is born of the dynamics of either: "Want-It-But-Can't-Have-It" or "Differences."

Want-It-But-Can't-Have-It: Take two characters that are in love and make it so their love simply cannot be (due to distance, circumstances or life issues). Put them in a room.

Examples of Want-it-But-Can't-Have-It

- Man is in love with his brother's wife.
- Nun who realizes she has feelings for a member of her church.
- An Israeli boy and a Palestinian girl fall for one another during a summer vacation.

Differences: Take two people who piss each other off, yet are extremely attracted to one another. Deep down they "get" one another and see through any masks or games.

Examples of Differences

- A natural-born liar and a squeaky-clean daughter of a minister.
- An old male chauvinist and a highly political feminist.
- A southern gentleman and a loud, ballsy New Yorker.

Onward track builders! Just one plank at a time.

Worksheet for Effective Scene Writing

Ask, does this scene have

GROUNDING: (Where are we? Who is there? Whose eyes are we looking through? Where are we physically: outside/inside? What is the year? (Time/Date) Any other information: Is it raining, snowing, a holiday or special event?)

_____

_____

_____

CONFLICT: (Does this scene have conflict, dramatic tension, suspense? What are the stakes and/or can the stakes be raised? Am I keeping the tension high until the very end?)

_____

_____

_____

PURPOSE/FORWARD MOTION: (What is the point of the scene? Why do I think this scene belongs in the story? How does this scene move the story forward or reveal character information? Is it a repeat of old information? DO YOU, the author, know why the scene is there?)

_____

_____

_____

SHOWING: (Would dialogue help bring this moment to life? Think of using the senses: How did things look, feel, taste, smell or sound? Any colors or music? What was the weather like? Are any symbols used? Is there an image that represents a larger idea in the book? What is the overriding emotion of the moment? Are you utilizing contrast?)

_____

_____

_____

SHAPE: (Does your character have a short-term goal? Does he or she meet with success, failure or a complication?)

_____

_____

_____

Takeaway Lessons for Tool #6 Writing the Compelling SCENE

- To make a great scene, you need to have Grounding, Conflict, Purpose/Forward Motion, Showing and Shape.
- You don't need to ground in every scene. If you told us in the last scene, that's good enough.
- You don't need high conflict in every scene. Some scenes serve to release the tension of the piece. Mix it up. Just don't let your protagonist out of trouble until the end.
- The shape of a scene involves your protagonist having a short-term goal. He or she then meets either with success, failure or a complication.
- Sequels come after scenes. (They are like mini-scenes.) And in these moments, the protagonist processes what just happened and decides what to do next. Think: Feelings → Options → New (Short-term) Goal

$$\text{Sequels} = F \rightarrow O \rightarrow N$$
$$\text{Feel} \rightarrow \text{Options} \rightarrow \text{New Goal}$$

Now, armed with this new goal, your protagonist will get that goal, fail or face a complication and on and on.

TOOL #7

Defining (and Using) Your VOICE Uncovering the Soul of Your Work

What You Have Done So Far

Tool #1: By figuring out where you write best, how you write best and by creating a nurturing place to write, you have given yourself the best chance at writing success.

Tool #2: By working to craft a solid story idea and theme, you've laid a solid foundation upon which to build your story. You know what you're writing and why you're writing it.

Tool #3: By traveling through the 9 Character Elements, you have added compelling characters to your creative stew.

Tool #4: By coming up with your 3 Key Spots, you've created the basic shape of your story.

Tool #5: By learning about outlining, you've begun to understand the major beats necessary in a plot. You've learned the dance that is plotting and pouring.

Tool #6: By learning how to craft a scene, you're learning how to breathe life into the small moments of a story to make it do a little tap dance.

"Don't Send Me Anything With Unicorns."

That's what the agent said when I told her that some of my clients were almost finished with their books. I had known this agent for a while. We were sitting at a table at a crowded writer's conference, sucking down coffee to stay alert. She leaned in and said, "I trust your judgment, but I just can't read another freaking unicorn story." She was an agent for Fantasy/YA books, and for some reason she had been barraged with a host of stories where a unicorn was somehow the key to unlocking the magic of the kingdom.

About six months later, I heard from a friend that this very same agent had taken on—believe it or not—a book whose main character befriends a magical unicorn that—believe it or not—is the key to unlocking the magic of the kingdom. So I called her up.

"So, what's the story? What was all that about no unicorns?"

"Yeah, I know. I didn't want to read it, but my assistant said that the voice was amazing. Unique, clear, fresh. So I read the first page, and I couldn't put the damn thing down. I swear if that woman wrote about snail races, I'd probably want to read it."

That, my friends, is the power of voice.

A strong voice can take any subject matter and bring it to life. I once read a short piece on sneezing that was so hilarious I went around quoting it for weeks. That author had made sneezing funny, compelling and a very worthwhile read. Now I'm not suggesting that you don't listen to the preferences of agents or that you try to take mundane subject matter and make it wonderful with your ability as a wordsmith. I'm just saying that knowing your voice, using your voice and *trusting your voice:* It's nothing to sneeze at.

A unique author's voice has the ability to make a reader feel a sense of intimacy and immediacy. A unique author's voice is a powerful weapon. And you should have that weapon in your… well, wherever it is that people keep weapons. (My son just yelled at me that it's called a cache.)

So, I'm about to write a bunch about voice that will definitely help, but if you're bored and want to skip to the point, here it is:

> # Risk Your Truth
> (It's as easy and as complicated as that.)

If that doesn't answer all of your questions on voice, then let's continue. We are going to cover some tools to explore your voice, give you a little kick in the pants to trust your voice and offer you some specific tools to be able to define your voice.

Q: How do you know when you've been able to define your voice?

A: You will be able to describe your author's voice in three words or less.

Q: Why is it important to define your writing voice?

A: Once you know it, you can claim it and take off as an original.

TERMS TO KNOW

Author's Voice: Is your overall voice; how your work might be described on the back of the book.

Voice of the Piece: The tone of one piece of work.

My Name Is Mittens and I'm Totally Confused

I was teaching at a conference about a year ago, and a young Texan woman at the back of the room delicately raised her hand. She declared that her name was Mittens and she was supremely confused when it came to voice. (Sidebar: I'm not entirely sure that was her name. But I swear it's what I heard.)

"When you say voice, do you mean the voice of the particular piece you're writing or the voice of the author?" she asked.

"Yes," I said.

"Okay, now I'm super confused."

I explained that voice could apply to both of these items.

When people discuss voice in writing, they are often referring to two different kinds of voice:

1. The overall voice of the author.
2. The voice of the piece you are writing/have written.

What I'm mostly concerned about (and what I'm going to spend the bulk of these pages talking about) is point number one: the voice of the author.

Overall Voice of the Author

It's not always easy to define an author's "voice," but you know it when you read it. In fact, many readers come to count on it. A reader may read one author if they want to laugh, another author if they crave biting political commentary, another if they're seeking a smart thrill ride. Voice involves the author's lens: The color with which they view the world.

When agents say they really like the author's voice, it often means that the writer is very clear about their point of view on life.

Some authors see the world through a dark, twisted lens.

Some authors see the world through a fact-based, no-nonsense lens.

Some authors see the world as depressing and troubling.

Some authors see the world as comical, wacky and weird.

Author's Voice

- Feels authentic to that author.
- Feels unique to that author.
- Often involves the author revealing him or herself.
- Often involves a level of risk taking.
- Often occurs when a writer is "in the flow."
- Often reveals the writer's passions and beliefs.

"Your voice is all about honesty... It's a process of peeling away the layers of your false self, your trying-to-be-something-you're-not self, your copycat self, your trying-to-sound-a-certain-way self, your spent-my-life-watching-television self." —Rachel Gardner, agent

Students will often ask me, how do I find my author's voice?

Okay, here's the deal. It's not a matter of finding it. You already have it. Truth be told, it's really a matter of learning to TRUST your voice.

It's a matter of turning up the volume.

For example, I once had a client, Susan, who was generally very polite and sweet. When another classmate asked her opinion, Susan would often politely shrug or go with the dominant feeling of the class. She was raised to follow "societal standards" as she called it. While she would come up with good story ideas, her material seemed to fall flat. Then one night, right before class, a big political world event occurred. It was something that got everyone talking. It became so compelling a discussion that we chucked what was on the syllabus that night and we talked—for real. It was on that night that I got to know Susan. I found out that she was actually quite feisty, funny and subversive. She had opinions! I told her to let them out on the page. I told her to turn the volume up on "feisty." Once she did that, her writing took on a sparkle that was all her own. It was awesome to watch.

Don't Be Afraid to

- Show off your personality.
- Use your sense of humor.
- Reveal your insecurities, flaws or imperfections.
- Be authentic.
- Be vulnerable.
- Reveal your passion.

I Encourage You to

- Read, watch, study and talk to other artists who risk on a regular basis.
- Cultivate silence.
- Try a "Radical Honesty" day. Pick a day when you're going to tell the absolute truth in your writing. You can always decide to toss it. (But don't, it's probably some of your best stuff.)

Listen, Play and Watch Out for Shame

As you uncover and begin to trust your voice, the healthiest and most productive way to approach this experience is to:

- Listen more.
- Play more.
- And watch out for shame.

Listen More

It may sound simple, but the dang truth is that if you can quiet your mind long enough to listen, I have no doubt at all that you will begin to hear your voice.

Spend time with your writing.

Listen to your story. Create an opening.

Your voice will start talking to you when you offer it space. It's like any good relationship. Invest in it and it becomes more alive.

Susanne Davis, writing coach and author, discusses voice as a combination of sound and silence:

> "In silence we allow ourselves first to be guided. Meditation and connections with nature help me. When I become silent, sound emerges to show me connection.

The wind and the birds herald in the seasons; whimsy and fury connect me to the truth of life's depth, and authentic characters stir to life."

Adopt a Playful Attitude

Time to play. That's right. I am officially giving you permission to play! As you explore your voice, try adding in a little playtime.

A few things you might not know about play:

- Adults need play just as much as children.
- We are hardwired to play.
- Play stimulates our brains.
- Our brains need it to invent material.
- Play assists with memory.
- Play assists with brainstorming.
- Play assists in silencing the inner critic.
- Play is essential to adaptability, emotional resilience and creativity.
- Play deficit can look a lot like sleep deficit.

So here I am, commanding you to play.

What is your play personality? Dr. Stuart Brown, author of *Play: How it Shapes the Brain, Opens the Imagination, and Invigorates the Soul*, reveals eight types:

1. The Explorer (physical or emotional searching and discovery)
2. The Competitor (enjoys competitive play, feels euphoria at winning)
3. The Joker (silly, goofy, nonsense fun)
4. The Director (enjoys planning and executing events and scenes)

5. The Creator/Artist (joy is found in making things)
6. The Kinesthete (likes to move, may need to move in order to think)
7. The Storyteller (loves to bring the written word to life)
8. The Collector (loves to have the best, most fascinating or diverse collection)

You may be one or several of these personality types.

What I have found is that while writing (being the storyteller), you may need to adopt a complementary style of play such as moving, exploring or collecting. Integrating other types of play into your writing routine keeps the writing fresh, the imagination moving and the ideas innovative.

Play with

1. Writing to music.
2. Switching narrators or points of view.
3. Switching tenses.
4. A new genre.
5. Writing from your antagonist's point of view.
6. Writing as your character at age 7.
7. Reading other authors—all different kinds of authors.
8. Watching movies or plays you'd normally never go see.
9. Reading a graphic novel.
10. Listening to music and noticing the voice in each song. Does the voice in the song sound like everyone else out there, or does it stand out to you in some way? If it stands out, why is it unique?
11. Voice exercises like the Free Word Grab which follows on Page 278.

Warning! Watch Out for Shame and Fear.

Once you are on the path to uncovering your voice, a few nasty beasts (fear and shame) are most likely going to try to pay you a visit. These beasts may try to distract you—or worse, they may try to suppress your voice.

Trusting your voice often means facing down and letting go of shame. This is an easy process for some but not for most. It requires practice. Many writers release shame in layers, one layer at a time, until their pure voice rises to the top.

> *"The secret killer of innovation is shame. You can't measure it, but it's there. Every time someone holds back on a new idea, fails to give their manager much-needed feedback and is afraid to speak up… you can be sure shame played a part."* —Peter Sheahan, author, speaker and CEO of ChangeLabs

Face Down Shame

My argument is that we are all very flawed. And so what?

What if we just acknowledged that we were flawed, lacking, sometimes scared and struggling? Would people self-medicate less? What if we lived in a society where we weren't trying to hide our pain, our flaws or our shortcomings? We might experience more peace.

I believe we are living in a time when it's becoming more acceptable to be vulnerable. I am noticing a trend where people are owning their ability to be vulnerable as a strength, not a weakness.

It's not your flaws that stop you. It's the shame that comes with them. What if you just dropped the shame?

Q: What if I've gotten all quiet and listened and faced down shame but I still don't know how to describe my author's voice?

A: Follow these steps:

DIG → MIX → LAUNCH
3 Steps to Finding (and Using) Your Voice

Step #1 → **Dig** (Pull up some weeds and play a little in the dirt.)

Time to excavate.

Look at your story.

Your voice partially comes from the story of you. How you were raised, where you were raised, your influences growing up, your good and bad experiences.

For example: A gritty, tough, biting voice stemmed from a writer I worked with who spent six years as a teenager living on the streets of Chicago.

A neurotic, humorous, intellectual voice came from a writer I worked with who was raised in New York by powerful, pressuring (you must get a Ph.D.!) parents.

Does voice always correlate to background experience? Not always. (But yeah, mostly.) In other words: It's a great place to start if you're not sure what kind of voice you may have.

Try asking yourself:

- Where was I raised?
- How was I raised?

→ Good parts of my upbringing: influences, experiences, accomplishments.
→ Not-so-good parts of my upbringing: struggles, difficult realities, wound.

First, let's discuss the good stuff.

Good Parts of My Upbringing/My Influences

- What did you grow up watching and listening to? Who were your biggest influences then?
- Who are you influences today? (Bukowski, Woody Allen, David Sedaris, Judy Blume, Steven King, Toni Morrison, Maya Angelou, Hemingway, Edgar Allen Poe?)

Influences Can Lead to Delightful Imitation

Many writers start out imitating other writers. There is nothing wrong with this at all. You read a book you love, see a play or a movie and think: *I want to do that!* So you try to do that. Usually the writing will have elements unique to you and elements of imitation. As you begin to know, understand and trust your voice, you will begin to separate from other artists. As you grow in confidence, you will begin to take risks—risks that reveal both the beauty and the shadow within. It is my belief that when an author is willing to reveal everything, to leave it all on the page, something unique happens. The writing takes on a life of its own.

My advice: Imitate and pay special attention when your voice asks you to make detours.

Not-So-Good Parts of My Upbringing: What Is My Wound?

The next step in digging is to look at your wound.

Q: Ummm, why do I have to look back on some crappy parts of my life?

A: Because

YOUR VOICE (*gift*) MAY BE RIGHT NEXT TO THE WOUND:

1. Life hurts us all; there's simply no way to get out unscathed. But the beauty of life is that the gift, what you have to give to the world, is often located—you guessed it—right next to that damn wound.
2. What I have found: The more familiar you are with your wound, the more you have talked about it and dealt with it, the less power it has over you. It's just part of your story.

Examples: Kim and Rick

Kim had a troubled childhood. She was raised by a single dad who was heavily addicted to meth. In fact, he was the first one who offered it to her. Needless to say, Kim experienced a long battle with drugs and alcohol herself. Once clean, she became a writer who led support groups for abused teens in their first week of rehab.

> Wound → Troubled childhood, raised by drug addict.
> Gift → Ability to empathize and care for others who struggle with addicts/addiction.

Rick grew up in a depressed, fearful household. His mother battled severe depression, sometimes not getting out of bed for weeks. Humor became his lifeline. He used humor to cheer up his mother, brothers and sisters. He is now a successful comedic actor and writer.

> Wound → Growing up in a severely depressed household.
> Gift → Ability to find laughter (even in the darkest moments) and provide it to others.

Okay, your turn. Look at your wound. Is your gift right next to it?

Let's brainstorm:

- What sucked in my childhood?
- How did I learn to cope with it?
- What gift came out of that period of struggle?
- How might these experiences have impacted my writer's voice?
- In what ways might my gift be right next to my wound?

_____

_____

_____

Play Exercise: The Free Word Grab

Don't think too much. Be playful and light and just circle words that pop out to you. I've noticed that this exercise works best when you meditate first or get relaxed and then play with combinations. Sometimes at writing retreats, I cut all these words up and put them on a large table and let the writers peruse. (Feel free to cut up this book!) Pick as many words as you want, but you will eventually settle on a combination of two or three.

Wild Serious Angry Erotic Fresh
Honest Seasoned Eccentric Dreamy Dark Funny
Loud Hip Sarcastic Violent Knowledgeable Worldly
Smooth Wacky Quirky Political Sensual Profound
Magical Rational Sweet Anxious Rebellious Pushy
Entertaining Vulnerable Cyber-punk Shocking Off-beat
Poetic Nerdy Romantic Fantastical Poignant Soulful
Feisty Spooky Cheerful New-age Lonely
Silly Artsy Soft Haunting Visionary Rude
Spontaneous Magical Coy Paranoid Lecherous Sexual
Aggressive Steamy Stubborn Easy-Going Superior
Irresponsible Sincere Uplifting Mysterious Spiritual
Powerful Pure Feminine Thrilling Charming
Risky Spiritual Light-hearted Temperamental Passionate Hysterical
Creative Old-Fashioned Human Cerebral Masculine Biting
Adventurous Youthful Compelling Soft Wise Intimate
Crafty Unpredictable Tense Child-like Chaotic Uplifting Innovative
Perceptive Cutting Intense Saucy Playful Grave
Self-effacing Racial Sardonic Friendly Innocent
Tell-it-like-it-is Wild Delightful Immature Whimsical
Flirtatious Rich Candid Witty Expert Grumpy Sly

Note: If you didn't see the word you want, just fill in one of the blanks with your word.

_____ _____ _____ _____

_____ _____ _____ _____

Step #2 → Mix

It's time to synthesize. You need a personal logline (or short pitch) that expresses your voice in three words or a sentence. Brevity means clarity.

So

1. **Look at all the words** you selected.
2. From that selection, **narrow it down to two or three**.
3. **Mix 'em up** to see what combination fits best. (To do this, I suggest writing the top three words on scraps of paper and looking at them in different combinations.) Don't censor yourself.

Here are some examples of how writers described their voices after doing the digging and mixing work:

Sarcastic-Witty-Fresh
Poetic-Lonely-Magical
Erotic-Innovative-Playful
Visionary–Haunting
Coy-Flirtatious–Feminine
Profound–Dreamy
Artsy-Lecherous-Haunting
Playful-Intelligent-Delightful
Thrilling-Risky
Tell-it-like-it-is–Rebellious
Quirky–Self-effacing
Mysterious-Spiritual-Thrilling
Raw-Emotional-Masculine

Step #3 → Launch

Time to use your voice! This can be scary. I use the term "launch" because of Sharon, a promising, talented writer I worked with a few years back when she had recently found her voice. One day, she called me up and told me that yeah, she may have found her voice, but she simply "was not going to use it." When I asked her why, she told me that it would require her to nearly learn how to fly in outer space—to launch herself into the unknown, to take the biggest risk of her life. So she didn't use it. No launching for approximately two years. Then she called me up and said, "Read what I just sent you." I read her piece and there it was—the writing was risky and magnificent—she was doing a skywalk with her full astronaut suit on.

"So what made you change your mind?" I asked.

"Two things. For one, I was getting older every day, and two, the voice that wanted me to be my true self became louder than the one that was afraid."

Living your voice is not always easy, but it's what sets you apart from any other writer. It's what can make you stand out in all of your glorious spectacular-ness.

Go walking in space.

Practical methods to use when launching your voice:

- → A "Radical Honesty" day.
- → Risking daily.
- → Using the Phases of Transformation.
- → Practicing standing in the light of your truth.

Radical Honesty Day

For every piece I write, I take an entire writing session to be radically honest about the characters, about the theme, about the storyline, about my flaws and faults and where they play into the piece: everything. I may never use a word of this work, but somehow getting this out of the way frees me up to be more honest in general. (The honest truth, by the way, is that I often do use this work.)

Keep RISK a Daily Experience:

Get Naked → be honest, be raw, be vulnerable.

Go Deep → go to the places you don't want to go.

Be Bold → go the places others won't go.

Why it's hard to risk: _____
_____

Why it's important to risk: _____
_____

How Risking Can Elevate Your Craft

No matter who you are or what you're writing about, I can tell you one thing for sure.

You've put a box around yourself and told yourself that you can only go so far.

Why do I know this for sure?

Because we all do it. Even if we are risk-takers, we've still put some artificial limit around us. (I call it a self-imposed horizon.)

When I started this book, I screwed up.

I forgot to put myself in it. My voice. It was a very technical book and had many references to Aristotle and Seneca and Shakespeare. But I'm in the classroom. I'm at the table. I work with writers every day. The way I reach a writer is not with a discussion of Aristotelian theory. It's with stories.

After one class on character, Suzanne, a "New-Yorky" writer came up to me and said she found that she was learning while being entertained. "Why do you find my class entertaining?" I asked. I truly had no idea and wanted to know.

She said, "Because we never know what you're going to say and, I guess, you say things we want to say but would never actually say out loud."

This started a discussion among all the thinkers and writers I knew about how most people want to say what they really feel but, most often, they don't. We don't want to stand out, be wrong, hurt others or be vulnerable. (But sometimes we have to.)

Voice, you see, is married to risk.

When you're ready to risk, your true voice will emerge.

Practice Standing in the Light of Your Truth

About a year ago, I was leading a 21-Day Writing Prompt Marathon (I send out writing prompts and little messages of inspiration for 21 days). I went on and on in class, in blog posts, in seminars and lectures about taking risks. One of my students (often being the teachers they are) innocently asked me about the last time I had risked and what I had written about. Arrrgh, right to the heart.

I hadn't risked in a long time and, truth be told, though I wanted very much to write about my experiences, I was in no state of mind to risk. Six weeks prior, I had lost a baby at five months of pregnancy. I had to go to the hospital and deliver a baby I knew would not live. It was horrifying. What followed were a depression and a PTSD response I had never in my life experienced. My mind, body and soul were trying to process all of the information. I wanted to write about it, but I was oddly frozen and scared.

Yet, her question stayed with me all the way home. Words rushed to my mind, phrases began to spring to life—and I quickly suppressed them. I did that until I realized I was doing what I told others not to do: Squashing my voice out of fear. And so I wrote a post about my experience. I wrote about the fear; I wrote about the loss and I wrote about the courage it was taking me to get up every day. I wrote about the nurse who talked about *Duck Dynasty* to keep me in good spirits. I wrote about my husband and best friend staying up for three days straight because everything that could go wrong in that hospital did go wrong. I opened up my heart in that post. And it wasn't easy.

The result was interesting. Most people responded favorably. They applauded my bravery and willingness to expose my darkest moment: My humanity and all that crap. But there were a few who didn't like it at all—to put it mildly. They had always seen me as a positive, upbeat person, and they didn't like how much darkness I had revealed. Some thought that as a teacher, I shouldn't have shown so much vulnerability that they considered to be weakness.

I was heartened by the warm responses and initially heartbroken by the criticisms. I decided to let it all sink in.

A few days later, I came home after work and my neighbor (who often leaves us cool stuff from his garden) had left us a pile of these huge orange-ish lemons.

I brought them inside, and my son yelled, "Let's make lemonade!" It was dusk and the sun was hanging low in the sky. I remember everything about that late afternoon because, although it was a small moment, it was life changing. As we squeezed the lemons and added the sugar, I found myself filling with an odd sense of gratitude. I had survived judgment. I found I was actually grateful to the "critiquers." We drank the lemonade and sat in our garden watching the bees. As the sun set, it bathed the garden in an orange-yellow glow. In that glow I realized:

- I had exposed myself.
- And some people had judged me harshly.
- And I was okay.

I had stood in the light of my own truth. And it was remarkably freeing.

Standing in the light of your own truth is not about waiting for rejection or receiving applause or waiting for any kind of reaction at all. It's about being who you are—*authentically*—regardless of the outcome.

You may experience judgment.

You may also experience an orange-lemon sunset.

Fail Big

Over the years of analyzing thousands of stories, I have anecdotally come to realize that the number-one character arc for protagonists is *lack of self-acceptance to self-acceptance*. (For example: Dorothy's character arc.) I would even go so far as to say that between 90 to 95 percent of protagonists with positive character arcs fall into this category. I believe the reason for this is that it may just be nearly every human being's inward struggle. So you're not alone. (And if you have a character with this character arc, then chances are you're on the right path.)

Recently, I went to a workshop with one of the best writing guides out there, John Vorhaus. If you don't have one of his books, go out and get one. Well, I bought his next book and he signed it for me.

Inside he wrote, *Fail Big*.

This was a big deal for me. And let me tell you why. Every writer wonders if they're fooling themselves, if they can succeed. Writers worry about putting themselves out there. *If it doesn't work, then what?*

The truth is that yes, you could put yourself out there and it could flop. But in that case, you'd be your tenacious self, look at the lessons you learned and try again. The truth is that your current writing could also touch people and speak to people and find its perfect audience. You don't know, and you won't know till you lift yourself up and toss your hat in the ring. So if you're going to put yourself out there, don't walk into the center ring timidly and softly. Announce your act. Walk into the center ring and carry that top hat proudly and speak into the microphone with confidence. Fail big, live big and succeed big. Believe in your ability to be: big.

Limited, Expanded and Free Voice

Finding your voice has a lot to do with expanding your parameters. Imagine you are a dog enclosed in a fence. The dog running around is your <u>limited</u> voice.

What if you took down the fence and pushed it back a little, you know, let the dog run freer with a little more space. This is your <u>expanded</u> voice.

Now what if you let the dog run totally wild and free? This is your pure, uninhibited <u>free voice</u>. You want to get there. You want to run free. You can always come back to the yard—just take a little joy run every now and then.

You have your truth. You know your truth. Are you speaking it?

Are you saying what you really think or are you writing what you think others want to hear?

This is a big question, and one I hope you take to heart.

It's a risk, I know. But it's often the reason you are called to write because you need to speak your truth.

Which brings me to my next point: Question success. We put ourselves in these confines of what it means to succeed and fail, what it means to be valuable in society, what it means if we don't do things the way others expect us to.

Question that.

Ask: Am I putting myself in a box I don't need to be in? Is this really reality, or is this a version I have sold myself? Am I limiting myself because I think that's "just the way it is?"

What We Tell Ourselves, What We Tell Each Other

I hear statements like this all the time:

"I'm not a bestselling kind of writer."

"I can't really say that."

"I can't write in that genre."

"I can't be that honest."

"I can't self-publish."

"I can't get an agent."

"I can't write dialogue."

"I can't be funny."

"I can't make a living as a writer."

Are you sure?

Question the version of reality you're selling yourself.

Now, let's take a moment to talk about the voice of the individual piece you're writing.

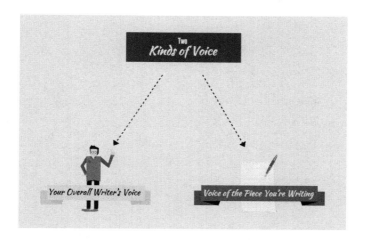

Voice of the Piece You're Writing

Let's get back to Mittens, the Texan writer I met at the conference. Mittens, as it turned out, considered herself a simple, down-to-earth country gal. Before writing full time, she had worked on a ranch. She had a blog about her heroic horses (they really were impressive), and she had published a memoir. Her writer's voice was honest, real and charmingly to-the-point. However, recently Mittens was trying on a new style of writing. She was writing a New Adult piece about a Las Vegas Madam. For this particular book, she was cultivating a voice that was raw, sexual and fierce.

While your overall writing probably has some definitive markers (that you may or may not be aware of), you can and should try on new voices as you attempt new genres, moods and styles. You can have a different voice for each piece you write, or you may be the kind of writer whose distinct voice permeates all of your work.

Important note: The voice of the piece you are writing will want to speak to you. So make sure to listen up.

Example

Lindsey was writing a book of short stories. Each one was written using a different point of view. One was from a traditional man from Oklahoma (the voice was gentle and challenging). One was from a black woman working in an agency (biting, satirical). One was about a young American couple who cared more for things than people in need (tragic, funny). On the surface, it looked like she was jumping around: Each piece she was writing had a unique voice.

Yet, when you looked at the collection, you could still hear her overall writer's voice: satirical and insightful with biting comments on human nature and our failings.

How Do I Discover the Voice of the Piece?

The voice of your story is the human thread, the underlying emotion and the emotional driving force.

You, as a writer, are speaking about the human condition. You are saying something that many people want to express but don't know how. You are speaking for people who aren't communicators.

Think about your story, the characters and the world they inhabit and then question:

- What fascinates you or inspires you about the people in your story? What about their behavior?
- What intrigues you about their society or culture?

- What issues in this piece make you angry or make you want to speak out?
- What issues in this piece make you upset, make you want to make things better?
- What issues in this piece scare you and keep you up at night?
- What motivates you, makes you want to get up in the morning to write this piece?

Each story you tell, whether you know it or not, is alive in its own way. It has its own heartbeat, its own voice.

Questions to find the voice (or heartbeat) of your story:

1. The protagonist is struggling with: _____
2. Society's current point of view on this issue: _____
3. My point of view on this issue: _____
4. My deepest hope about this issue: _____
5. My deepest fear about this issue: _____

Example #1: Toni is writing a memoir about her mother's struggle with Alzheimer's.

1. The protagonist is struggling with: *Mom with Alzheimer's.*
2. Society's current point of view on this issue: *We don't want to see it. It scares us.*
3. My point of view on this issue: *It's the cruelest thing I've ever seen.*
4. My deepest hope about this issue: *There will be a cure soon.*
5. My deepest fear about this issue: *That I face it myself.*

Example #2: Anastasia is writing a political thriller about the NSA's information gathering techniques.

- The protagonist is struggling with: *How much our government monitors our lives.*
- Society's current point of view on this issue: *mixed. Some feel we need this much monitoring to keep terrorism at bay. Others are outraged by it.*
- My point of view on this issue: *I don't trust politicians, so I don't trust the people gathering the information, so this trend scares the living daylights out of me.*
- My deepest hope about this issue: *More transparency so the people can be aware of what's going on (and protest if need be).*
- My deepest fear about this issue: *We no longer have privacy and never will again.*

Use the 5-Step "Phases of Transformation" Process:

If you'd like to use the Phases of Transformation as a process to begin to trust your voice, here's an example:

Roxzana, a Fairly New Writer

1. **SEE IT. Pick a goal:** *Trust my voice.*
2. **Connect with Source/Make Space:**
   While going for a daily walk, I ask for assistance to be able to trust my voice. My main struggle is that I doubt my own voice. My inner critic is so loud, I doubt almost every sentence.
3. **Grab Your Shadow; It's Coming Too:**
   Self-doubt is my shadow. It's coming with me, but it won't stop me. As I thought about it on my walks, I realized that I was often

hearing my father's voice in my head when I wanted to write. I felt he wouldn't approve of my writing. In fact, I knew he wouldn't.

4. **Enter the Discomfort:**
   As I began to write, I found I was experiencing more than discomfort. I would only allow my voice to come through for a few minutes at a time. I did some exercises and found my voice to be sultry, poetic and a little bit wild. I was not raised to be any of these things! Every time I felt I was letting out my sultry side, I would clutch up. I tried to push through it because I was beginning to understand that I needed to feel this clutched up to grow.

5. **Allow and Applaud the Transformation:**
   I was definitely choking and, at the same time, I was definitely doing some writing. The first time I wrote an entire page in my voice, a large part of me was dismissive. I remember thinking, "It's just a page." Then again, I had never written so much in my voice before. I had never been that daring—that sexual. It was a first. I did my best to feel good about the work I had done. Thankfully, my writing group loved my work, and that helped.

My goal was to write one short story in my voice. It wasn't easy. I would lapse in and out of taking risks, which meant I lapsed in and out of trusting my voice. I made a goal with my writing group to complete my story in three weeks. I wrote best in the morning, after my walk. It took me eight weeks (I know, I know), but I finally completed it. That first short story in my voice was the hardest. After that, it got a little easier. I made the new goal of writing a collection of stories. With each story, I found I got a little bolder. At times, I would still clutch up, but ironically I found I was almost craving the moments of honesty. I wanted that connection more than anything else.

How Other Writers Find Their Voices:

"I think your voice finds you, just like that stray red dog, and your first house that had purple trim and a slanted living room floor, or your first guitar. These are things that speak to and come from your soul. And you'll know it when you hear it, sitting quietly with pen in hand, behind a closed door on a long afternoon, when all you have is you and the page and nothing but time." —Danielle

"As a writer of memoir, the biggest fear I face is what the family's reaction will be. What helps with that fear is writing down and posting the reasons why I need to write, the good it may do, the understanding it may provide, the change it may facilitate in the world. The second thing that helps is to write yes, honestly, but also with compassion and forgiveness. In fact, I have these three attributes posted on my wall, as well." —Shirley

"Prompt writing is a great way to find your voice. Free write for 10 minutes each day using a different prompt. After two weeks, read through your work and you'll see a common thread you've injected into all of those different themes. That will reveal your voice." —Brian

"I try to get myself out of the way." —Ed

Q: How do I know if I've found my voice?

A: Here are a few ways to tell:

- Your writing fills you with emotion; maybe it scares you or moves you or makes you laugh.
- Your writing looks, feels and sounds like you.
- You are risking and exposing yourself, exposing your own flaws.
- Your true beliefs are on the page. You are telling your truth.

A lot of times, writers write for the marketplace. This almost never works. You might sell, but you won't be communicating your voice.

Ask yourself: Am I writing what I truly want to say or writing what I think others want to read?

How honest am I being?

Am I taking risks?

If you knew you were dying in a week, what piece would you be writing today?

Worksheet to Uncover Your Writer's Voice

Goal: *Describe Your Voice in Three Words; Risk Your Truth!*

DIG: (Seek to learn your story. Check to see if your gift is next to your wound.)

Influences: _____

_____

Wound: _____

_____

Gift: _____

_____

How this experience/time period in my life impacted my writer's voice _____

_____

My lens tends to be: (humorous, thoughtful, outrageous, dramatic, satirical, poetic, edgy, sarcastic, horrifying, whimsical, dark, etc.) _____

How might others describe your writing? _____

Do the Free Word Grab exercise. Circle all the words that define your writer's voice.

MIX: (Narrow it down to TWO OR THREE WORDS)

    1. _____
    2. _____
    3. _____

LAUNCH: (Owning your voice is a lifestyle shift of trusting, risking and expressing tenaciously.)

How can I start to use my voice in my writing? _____

_____

How can I risk more? _____

_____

What would happen to my writing if I fully trusted my voice? _____

_____

If I were totally honest with my writing, I would write about _____

_____

_____

Takeaway Lessons for Tool #7 Defining and Using Your VOICE

1. Risk your truth. It's as simple and as complicated as that.

2. Steps to define and use your voice. Think: Dig, Mix and Launch!
   - Dig → Seek to learn your story. Uncover your influences and your wound. Check to see if your gift is next to your wound. How did your childhood experiences impact your writer's voice?
   - Mix → Synthesize it. Describe your voice in a few sentences/words. From the Free Word Grab, what words best describe you?
   - Launch → Owning your voice is a lifestyle shift of trusting, risking and expressing tenaciously. How can I start to use my voice in my writing? How can I risk more? What would happen to my writing if I fully trusted my voice?

3. No one can be you but you. You have a unique way of viewing the world, which is called your lens.

4. It's important to listen, to dive into the silence to turn up the volume on your voice.

5. Try a radical-honesty writing session. Even if you never reveal it to another soul, it's freeing.

6. Once you begin to hear your voice, do your best to trust it and to trust the fact that your voice is worthy of being expressed.

7. Experiment, play with writing styles, genres, voices and points of view—whatever and whenever—and have some fun.

8. Risking means facing down shame.

9. You can use the Phases of Transformation to work on finding and trusting your voice. If you experience some anxiety, you are probably on the right path.

In Conclusion...

Oh dear, God. Now what?

Though you may have heard me say it before, you may need to hear me say it again before you head off on your journey:

TENACITY: RINSE AND REPEAT

Okay, let me be frank with you. I have superpowers. I didn't want to tell you before because it sounds nuts. But here we are at the end of the book, so what the hell. I have two superpowers exactly, and they're extremely limited:

- I can often put a spell on people to help them break their writer's block, and
- I can gently but powerfully nudge people to uncover their passion and to make it their life's work.

If writing is your thing, if it's what you want to do more than anything else, then embrace tenacity and ride it for all it's worth. Think of me as a fairy godmother using her superpowers right now—on you.

It's not exactly an easy life—being a writer—but I know I wouldn't want any other life. I meet the most fascinating people, have the most interesting conversations and my mind and soul are always deliciously engaged in an exciting project. When you bring this kind of passion to your writing, and when you combine it with a tenacious spirit, you'll be a force to be reckoned with. You'll uncover superpowers of your own.

The time has come to stop hiding in the shadows and denying your brilliance. The time has come to act.

As you near the end of this book, you may experience some fear or anxiety. This is a good sign! Enter the discomfort. (It means you are growing.)

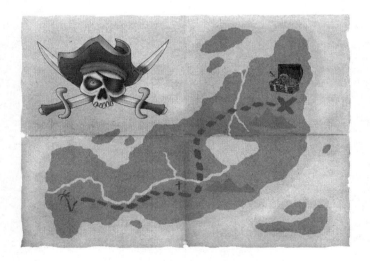

Remember the Pirate?

All he needed was a map, some sense of where he was headed and the willingness to let it all hang out. You have the map in your hands. If you ever get lost, take a deep breath and come back to a tool in the book that can address the issue that's vexing you. Don't worry about nailing every step perfectly. If the words don't come out the way you want them to, remember, they're just words and you can always rearrange them.

Just get into the silence: Listen for the direction, grab your playful spirit and go.

Go now. Write. Go!

"Never bend your head. Always hold it high. Look the world straight in the face." —Helen Keller

The End

Wait, one more thing.

Find the message that calls to you and tear along the dotted line. Put it up somewhere you'll see it and can repeat it to yourself daily:

....

I'm not sure how I will get it all done, but I'm 100% committed to finishing.

....

I am a writer. What I have to say is valid and important.

....

Risking and sharing my unique voice are signs of strength.

....

Perfection is never required.

....

If I hit a writing rough patch, I know I can get through it. Writing is filled with ups and downs. An up is coming.

....

My work will find its perfect audience.

....

Ideas are flowing to me easily and steadily. I am in my perfect creative space. I can find inspiration at any moment.

....

I know that small movements are important movements. I applaud every step on the journey, no matter how small it may seem.

....

I can visualize writing success. I have all the tenacity I need to actualize my dreams. I am a writing powerhouse.

....

Okay, I'm done now.

Except for this stuff.

Appendixes

1. Time Management for the Writer

2. More **15 Plot Spots Examples**: *Harry Potter and the Sorcerer's Stone, Pride and Prejudice* and *Thelma and Louise*

3. More Tools That I Couldn't Stuff Anywhere Else

   - World-Building Worksheet
   - Point of View Quick Go-To Guide
   - Techniques to Deepen Characters
   - Books I Used to Create My Methods of Madness

Appendix 1:

Troubleshooting a Common "Writerly" Issue

A bit about TIME MANAGEMENT

Q: What is Time Management?

A: It is the act or process of planning and exercising conscious control over the amount of time spent on specific activities, especially to increase effectiveness, efficiency or productivity.

Key words in this definition: CONSCIOUS CONTROL—when you become conscious, you can exert control over your time. If you are not sure whether you need some assistance with your time management, take the assessment test below:

Time Management Self-Assessment Test for the Writer

1. Do you utilize goal setting?   Yes   No
2. Do you make to-do lists?   Yes   No
3. Can you visualize your goals in detail?   Yes   No
4. Do you know where (home, coffee shop, library) you write best?   Yes   No
5. Do you have a method to tackle procrastination?   Yes   No

6. Do you have one or more people who help hold you accountable? Yes No
7. Do you know how (computer, long hand, with background noise) you write best? Yes No
8. Do you know what works to keep you motivated? Yes No
9. Do you have a method to silence your inner critic? Yes No
10. Do you know how to prioritize tasks? Yes No
11. Do you know when (time of day) you write best? Yes No
12. Do you set aside a few minutes to organize your time (for the week/day)? Yes No
13. Do you have a method for handling interruptions? Yes No
14. Are you 100 percent committed to finishing your first draft or rewrite? Yes No
15. Do you have a method to eliminate multitasking/create focused attention? Yes No
16. Do you utilize affirmations? Yes No
17. Do you have writing rituals that keep you motivated? Yes No
18. Do you feed your muse to keep yourself inspired to keep writing? Yes No
19. Do you have a reward method for when you complete small writing tasks? Yes No
20. Do you get enough sleep and eat healthy foods while writing? Yes No
21. Do you keep distractions (email/Facebook) to a minimum when you write? Yes No

How many times did you mark "Yes"_____?

How many times did you mark "No"_____?

If you had more than five "No's" then it's time to build up some time management muscles!

Concrete Time-Management Tools for the Writer

- De-clutter your writing space.
- Learn how to prioritize.
- Make a Sunday to-do list—prioritize!
- Make a daily to-do list—prioritize!
- Find your tools to limit procrastination.
- Find your tools to limit interruptions.
- Utilize deadlines.
- Create a writing routine that works for you.
- Utilize accountability partners/writing groups.
- Don't wait for inspiration.
- Stick to a regular writing time.

Time-Management Mistakes/What to Avoid

- Too many things on your to-do list.
- Multitasking.
- Checking emails, Facebook, tweeting (this interrupts your focus).
- Working in an environment where you often get interrupted.
- Leaving emails in your inbox (handle them when you read them).

Questions to ask to simplify your life and create a more effective writing practice:

- What event or activity in my business or personal life can I eliminate to make room for writing?
- What can I learn to say "no" to in my life?
- How can I feel calm enough to write even when I have a lot on my to-do list?

Tips to handle procrastination:

- Get organized (clear, inviting writing space).
- Write up a priority list every night for the next day.
- Make sure to put good stuff (the stuff you want to do) on your to-do list.
- Reward yourself for the amount of "to-dos" that got done.
- Step out of your comfort zone slowly—one step at a time—but keep moving.
- Utilize reminder notes (Post-its).
- Make sure your goals are realistic.
- Offer small rewards for completing tasks.
- Reward yourself for the moments that you do not procrastinate.
- Adopt the "dancing-tortoise" approach. Slow and steady progress—but dance along the way to instill a little daily joy.

My Personal Motivation Map

What you will need to create your own Motivation Map

1. Corkboard
2. Affirmations
3. Visual picture of short-term goal
4. Visual picture of long-term goal
5. "To do" this week (done every Sunday)

You can add anything else that motivates you! Power-thought cards, sayings, phrases, quotes, photos. Be creative. Keep your personal Motivation Map in a place where you will see it daily.

Appendix 2:

More 15 Plot Spots Examples: *Harry Potter and the Sorcerer's Stone, Pride and Prejudice* and *Thelma and Louise*

Example #1: **15 Essential Plot Spots of** *Harry Potter and the Sorcerer's Stone* by J.K. Rowling

1. The Grabber: Magical people everywhere are celebrating because the evil Lord Voldemort has been defeated by a baby named Harry Potter.

2. Old Self in Old World: Harry is downtrodden and mistreated by his horrible relatives, the Dursleys. He has no friends, and there is very little that's good about his life.

3. This Changes Everything/The Catalyst: Harry learns he has been accepted into Hogwarts School of Witchcraft and Wizardry.

4. Struggles and Prep: Harry learns he is a wizard and that his parents were also wizards, killed by Lord Voldemort. Voldemort attempted to kill Harry too, but something mysterious happened, and the spell recoiled on Voldemort, nearly destroying him. Harry is regarded as a hero by the wizarding world. Harry goes with Hagrid to obtain his school supplies in Diagon Alley. Hagrid withdraws a small package from Gringotts Bank.

——————————— End ACT 1 ———————————

─────────── ACT 2 Begins Here ───────────

5. Here We Go: Harry, left alone at King's Cross Station, has no idea how to get onto Platform 9 3/4, but with help from Mrs. Weasley, he finds his way to the Hogwarts train. He has now entered the wizarding world.

6. Rough Landing/Small Victories: Harry makes friends with Ron Weasley and becomes an enemy of Draco Malfoy. Harry and Ron are sorted into Gryffindor, the most prestigious house, but Snape, the Potions Master, seems to hate Harry. Harry learns that someone attempted to rob Gringotts Bank the same day that Hagrid withdrew the package and realizes that someone is trying to steal it. When Harry and his friends accidentally end up in a forbidden corridor, they meet a gigantic three-headed dog that guards a trapdoor, and they realize the package must be hidden beyond it. Harry and Ron become friends with Hermione when the three of them successfully fight an escaped cave troll.

7. The Gut: Snape's inexplicable hatred of Harry comes to a head when he attempts to hex Harry off his broom in Harry's first Quidditch match, which confirms Harry's growing fear that Snape is attempting to steal the mysterious package.

8. Do a Little Dance/Danger Looming: Harry, Ron and Hermione attempt to learn about the package in order to protect it from Snape. They learn that it is the Sorcerer's Stone and discover that Snape is bullying the nervous, stuttering Professor Quirrell. Harry and his friends believe it is only a matter of time before Quirrell breaks down and tells Snape how to get the Stone.

9. Revelation and/or Obstacle: Hagrid has been raising a baby dragon, which Harry and Hermione must help him get rid of. They are caught out of bed, losing 150 points for Gryffindor House and the good opinion of all the other students. Harry resolves not to interfere in things that don't concern him. Meanwhile, a creature has been murdering unicorns in the

Forbidden Forest. A centaur tells Harry that the person killing unicorns and seeking the Sorcerer's Stone is the semi-corporeal Lord Voldemort, attempting to regain his power.

──────────── End ACT 2 ────────────

──────────── ACT 3 Begins Here ────────────

10. The Mini Crisis: Harry discovers that Hagrid won the baby dragon in a game of cards, during which he revealed to a mysterious hooded figure how to get past the three-headed dog. The person seeking the Stone now knows everything he needs to reach it.

11. New Self Emerging: None of the teachers want to listen to his fears about the safety of the Stone or his suspicions about Snape, so Harry is determined to take the protection of the Stone into his own hands.

12. It's Not Looking Good: Dumbledore has left Hogwarts and will not be back until tomorrow. McGonagall, in charge during his absence, refuses to believe the Stone is in danger. Snape says if Harry is caught out of bed at night, he will personally make sure Harry is expelled.

13. Last Big Decision/Old vs. New Self: Now Harry resolves to go after the Stone himself to stop anyone from stealing it: Keeping it safe from Voldemort is more important than the risk of expulsion.

14. Climax: Harry, Ron and Hermione overcome a series of obstacles to reach the Stone, only to discover that the person attempting to steal it is not Snape but Quirrell, who is possessed by Voldemort. Harry obtains the Stone and grapples with Quirrell. When their skin touches, it burns them both, so to keep Quirrell from cursing him and escaping, Harry holds onto Quirrell until it nearly kills him.

15. The Wrap Up/The Ending: Harry wakes up in the hospital wing. Dumbledore tells him Voldemort has been prevented from returning and answers many of Harry's questions. Harry, Ron and Hermione's efforts to protect the Stone win Gryffindor the House Cup. Harry returns to the Dursleys knowing he will come back to Hogwarts next year.

Example #2: **15 Essential Plot Spots of** *Pride and Prejudice* by Jane Austen

1. The Grabber: A rich young man, Mr. Bingley, has rented a nearby estate, and Mrs. Bennet hopes he will marry one of her daughters.

2. Old Self in Old World: Elizabeth is the sharpest and cleverest of her sisters and enjoys mocking anyone she considers to deserve it.

3. This Changes Everything/The Catalyst: Jane Bennet and Mr. Bingley like each other immediately, but Mr. Bingley's proud and disagreeable friend, Mr. Darcy, insults Elizabeth Bennet.

4. Struggles and Prep: Though Elizabeth wishes only to marry someone she loves and respects, the entail on the Bennet estate means that the girls will be left almost penniless if they do not marry well. Unaware of Mr. Darcy's growing admiration for her, Elizabeth continues to mock him for what she perceives as his pride. Her dislike is fueled by her acquaintance with Mr. Wickham, who claims that Mr. Darcy unfairly wronged him.

———————— End ACT 1 ————————

———————— ACT 2 Begins Here ————————

5. Here We Go: During her dance with Mr. Darcy at the Netherfield Ball, Elizabeth gives vent to her anger at his alleged ill-treatment of Mr. Wickham. Darcy claims he did no wrong but will not discuss the subject in detail. Both leave angry though Darcy's feelings for Elizabeth outweigh his annoyance.

6. Rough Landing/Small Victories: The rest of the Bennet family, except for Jane, behaves horribly for the rest of the Netherfield Ball. Elizabeth refuses the marriage proposal of the odious Mr. Collins, but her best friend, Charlotte, accepts his hand. Bingley disappears to London, apparently by the design of his sisters, dashing Jane's hopes of marrying him. Things improve when Elizabeth leaves to visit the newly married Collinses. She is reconciled with Charlotte, amused by the interference of Lady Catherine de Bourgh and even begins to enjoy the company of Mr. Darcy and his cousin when they come. All this changes when she accidentally learns that Mr. Darcy congratulates himself for deliberately separating Mr. Bingley and Jane.

7. The Gut: Mr. Darcy asks Elizabeth to marry him. She refuses. In response to her accusations about his mistreatment of both Jane and Mr. Wickham, Mr. Darcy writes a letter explaining his actions, particularly Mr. Wickham's bad conduct and attempt to elope with Mr. Darcy's sister.

8. Do a Little Dance/Danger Looming: Elizabeth understands that her prejudice against Mr. Darcy was unfounded and excessive, and she gains a clearer perspective of the misbehavior of her family. Though she confronts her father about how he lets her youngest sister run wild, it does no good, and Lydia is allowed to visit the soldier encampment at Brighton in the company of some friends.

9. Revelation and/or Obstacle: When visiting with her aunt and uncle, Elizabeth visits Pemberley, Mr. Darcy's estate, and gets a much more positive impression of him from the people there. Mr. Darcy returns home unexpectedly and is friendlier to Elizabeth and her aunt and uncle than she has ever seen him be. He introduces her to his sister, and Elizabeth finds herself growing fond of him.

──────────── **End ACT 2** ────────────

──────────── **ACT 3 Begins Here** ────────────

10. The Mini Crisis: Elizabeth receives news from home that Lydia has run away with Mr. Wickham, which will ruin the family if he does not marry her. Mr. Darcy happens to find Elizabeth just as she learns this, and she tells him all of it.

11. New Self Emerging: Just as Elizabeth becomes certain that she can never marry Darcy, she discovers that she really loves him. Out of love for Elizabeth, Mr. Darcy overcomes his pride to bribe Wickham into marrying Lydia, which saves the Bennet family from disgrace.

12. It's Not Looking Good: Lydia and Wickham have run away to London and do not plan to marry. This will ruin Lydia's life and the family's reputation and destroy the Bennet girls' hopes of good marriages.

13. Last Big Decision/Old vs. New Self: Lady Catherine de Bourgh confronts Elizabeth to make her promise never to marry Mr. Darcy. Though Elizabeth assumes she has lost all hope of marrying him, she refuses to promise not to. This decision unites both the assertiveness she has always had with her newfound careful judgment and love of Mr. Darcy.

14. Climax: Elizabeth thanks Mr. Darcy for saving her family's reputation, and Darcy asks her to marry him. She accepts.

15. The Wrap Up/The Ending: Darcy and Elizabeth discuss and dispel their misunderstandings throughout the story. The main characters marry, and everyone lives as happily as their personalities will allow.

Example #3: **15 Essential Plot Spots of** *Thelma and Louise* **(Movie script written by Callie Khouri.)**

1. The Grabber: Opens on a black and white stretch of highway that leads off to a mountain; comes into color, then gets darker and darker until black.

Diner: Louise (Susan Sarandon) is a waitress serving in a busy diner. She tells people not to smoke; then she lights up in the back. Louise calls Thelma (Gina Davis). We are introduced to Thelma's controlling and demeaning husband, Daryl, who tells Thelma he will be working late on Friday night. We learn that Thelma and Louise are heading out for a girls' weekend in the mountains.

2. Old Self in Old World: Thelma is in a crappy marriage with a husband who ignores her (and is abusive when he doesn't ignore her). She is naive, controlled and lacking experience in life and love. Thelma packs everything, dumping her drawers out, bringing all of her clothes and fishing stuff, lanterns and her gun. She shoves it all into a huge suitcase. Louise is strong and stern yet jaded, having seen too much. We suspect she's carrying a traumatic event in her recent past. Louise packs neatly and selectively in clean plastic bags. Louise picks Thelma up in her Thunderbird. They take a pic and they are off—speeding down the highway. Thelma gives the gun to Louise. Thelma lights a cigarette—the beginnings of freedom!

3. This Changes Everything/The Catalyst: The two women stop at a bar where they drink a little and meet an overly friendly man named Harlan. Thelma, who just wants to have a little fun, orders a drink saying, "I've had it up to my ass with sedate. Look out, 'cause my hair is coming down." We learn that Louise is mad at her boyfriend, but we don't know why.

315

Harlan asks Thelma to dance. Thelma is elated. Louise is suspicious and a little uncomfortable. They are both drinking now. Thelma is dancing with Harlan, who is clearly getting a little too friendly. Louise is asked to dance. They are both having fun line dancing to a live band. Louise goes to the bathroom after telling Thelma that they will be leaving in a few minutes.

Thelma finds herself a little drunk and Harlan takes her outside for air. Once outside, he hits on her; she refuses and he gets violent. Thelma tries to break free. He pulls her skirt up; she tries to get away and he slaps her, ripping her dress. He starts to rape her. Louise comes out and pulls the gun on Harlan. Thelma gets up, crying. Harlan won't back down, they back up and she leaves. Harlan defiantly yells, "Suck my cock. Bitch, I should have gone ahead and f*#** her." Louise shoots him. He dies. Louise states, "You watch your mouth, buddy." Thelma gets in the car and they speed off.

4. Struggles and Prep: Louise has just killed a man. Thelma wants to go to the police, but Louise says, "No one will believe us." Her previous experiences with the law have shown her that her best option is to make a getaway. She gives Thelma the option of getting out and going home. Thelma chooses to stay with Louise.

―――――――――――― End ACT 1 ――――――――――――

―――――――――――― ACT 2 Begins Here ――――――――――――

5. Here We Go: Life as outlaws begins. On the road, now everything has changed. They are on their own and have to find out what to do next.

6. Rough Landing/Small Victories:

<u>Rough Landing</u>: They fight and blame one another for the situation they are in. Thelma calls home at 4 a.m. and Daryl is not home. Louise tries her boyfriend, Jimmy, but there is no answer. They are truly on their own.

Back at the parking lot of the bar, the police are taking Harlan's body away. They question the waitress about Thelma and Louise, trying to ID them. It is concluded that either they murdered Harlan or witnessed it.

Small Victories: They realize that no one saw the murder and that no one knows conclusively that it was them. Louise comes up with a plan; they will need money. She connects with Jimmy and asks him for help—to wire her life savings of $6,700. "I did something bad. Will you help me?" Jimmy says he'll help.

Challenge/Obstacle: The FBI is now after the women. They are on their way to Oklahoma City; then Louise is going to Mexico. She asks Thelma if she will come with her.

Situation: Jimmy confirms that he wired the money; it's under the name "Peaches."

Revelation: Thelma calls Daryl. She is supposed to tell him that she is having a good time and will be back tomorrow. He is such an ass that she tells him to f**# himself. (Thelma is finding her inner strength.)

Challenge/New Goal: Thelma commits to going to Mexico.

Situation: Thelma meets a cute cowboy traveler (Brad Pitt). Thelma wants to take him with them, but Louise says no.

Challenge/New Goal: They bust out the map. They need to get to Mexico without going through Texas. Something bad happened to Louise there. The police make their way to Louise's apartment to start their investigation.

Situation: They see the cute cowboy again. Thelma begs, and Louise agrees to let him come with them for a short while.

Revelation: We learn more about Thelma's history: She has been with Daryl since she was 14, they got married at 18 and she has never had sex with anyone else.

Obstacle/Challenge: They are confronted with a police roadblock and are forced to take another route. This is a clear reminder that the police are closing in.

7. The Gut: Love and Money: Louise goes to pick up the money and finds that Jimmy is there. Louise puts Thelma in charge of guarding the money overnight. They get hotel rooms. Jimmy and Louise fight initially. Jimmy proposes, she says no. Brad knocks on Thelma's door. She is nervous and unsure but lets him in. This is a tragedy, so it is a false victory. They seem to be in control here. They have the money and have a plan.

8. Do a Little Dance/Danger Looming: Night of Love and Sex: Intercut between Louise breaking up with Jimmy (telling him it's bad timing, they make love as a goodbye) with Brad and Thelma flirting (seducing one another and having the best sex of Thelma's life—hot, raw and wild).

Danger Looming: Brad is a professional thief who robs convenience stores. He shows off, demonstrating for Thelma how he performs his robberies, including what he says. His being an outlaw turns her on.

Challenge: Jimmy leaves, they say goodbye. He gives Louise the ring to keep.

9. Revelation and/or Obstacle:

Revelation: Thelma comes down to breakfast all sexed up. She just had the best sex of her life; she now understands more of what it means to be a woman. But she has left the cute cowboy alone with their money. Brad was the looming danger; he has stolen their money.

Obstacle: Their money is gone. Now, what?

─────────── End ACT 2 ───────────

─────────── ACT 3 Begins Here ───────────

10. The Mini Crisis: Louise loses it, and Thelma grabs the wheel. Louise breaks down fully and for the first time. Thelma tries to comfort her and says it's okay. But Louise has lost hope, saying it's not okay. She's a mess. Thelma takes charge, saying, "Don't you worry about it. Get your stuff, let's get out of here, move!"

11. It's Not Looking Good: The police are on the case and in hot pursuit. They set up a command center at Daryl's house and tap his phone. Thelma robs a convenience store using the tools she learned from the traveling cowboy. Louise is comatose. "DRIVE LOUISE! DRIVE!"

12. New Self Emerging: Now the two are seriously running for their lives; they have to make it to Mexico before the police find them.

The FBI watches Thelma's robbery on the camera from the convenience store. As they are driving for their lives, Thelma realizes she is on a high from the robbery, saying, "It's like I've been doing it all my life." Police track down Jimmy and try to get information from him. Louise sells her jewelry, asks Thelma to call Daryl.

The cute cowboy is picked up by the police and interviewed. The police find out that he stole money from Thelma and Louise. Thelma would not have committed the robbery if he hadn't taken all their money. Policeman: "They had a chance; now you screwed it up for them!"

Revelation: The police seem to know everything. Louise tells Thelma to call Daryl to see if he knows anything. On the call, Daryl is very nice to her. Thelma hangs up stating, "He knows." Louise calls Slocum (FBI man), and they learn the charges they are facing and that the FBI is aware of the plan to go to Mexico.

Revelation: Driving at night, with everything to lose, and yet they seem more in charge of their lives than they ever have been.

Situation: Chauvinistic trucker harasses them by making perverted gestures.

Revelation: Thelma figures out Louise was raped in Texas (even though she still won't talk about it).

Challenge/Obstacle: A lone police car pulls them over; they have to lock the policeman in the trunk (first making air holes) and take his ammo. They apologize for leaving him in the trunk.

Revelation: They may truly be facing death.

13. Last Big Decision/Old vs. New Self: Louise calls to talk with Agent Slocum. He tries to reach her, saying, "I know what's making you run, I know what happened to you in Texas." He truly understands and asks them to come in. "You will come in dead or alive." They decide not to turn themselves in.

Revelation: They can't go back. Thelma: "Something has crossed over in me and I can't go back." They are awake to their lives. Thelma: "I don't remember being this awake."

Challenge/Goal: To get to Mexico. They are both 100 percent committed now. The perverted trucker taunts them once again. They ask him to pull over and to apologize. He refuses and curses at them. They start shooting at his truck until they blow it up. They have taken off, but close behind are the police—at the scene of the truck explosion. The law is closing in faster and faster.

14. Climax: The police track them relentlessly until there is a high-speed chase. It's messy and filled with crashes: Police cars are flipping, crashing and spinning. As they flee, Thelma tells Louise that no matter what happens, "I'm glad I came with you." They no longer blame one another and see the journey as somewhat inevitable. There is no way out: Their car is being chased by 15 cop cars coming at them from all angles.

They have outrun the police momentarily, but it is clear they can't escape. A police helicopter looms overhead. It creates a huge dust storm so they don't exactly see what's ahead. The women come to a screeching halt and almost go off the cliff of the Grand Canyon. They take in its beauty. They see that this is where their road has been leading.

An army of loaded-gun-bearing policemen park and aim their guns at them. On the loudspeaker, the police demand they turn themselves in. Slocum sees the situation, feels it is overkill and will force the women to do something desperate. He tries to communicate this to his superior; it falls on deaf ears.

They decide to keep going. They don't want to get caught, go to jail and lose their lives that way. They cry and kiss. Slocum runs after them. Louise hits the gas pedal and their car races toward the cliff.

15. The Wrap Up/The Ending: Thelma and Louise hold hands as they head off the cliff. Close up on the snapshot they took at the beginning of their trip. The Polaroid flies off into the air; that moment is gone. Freeze-frame on the car flying over the cliff. Over triumphant music, we see images of their journey—happy ones of them smiling on the road trip that ended their lives.

Appendix 3

More Tools I Couldn't Stuff Anywhere Else

World-Building Worksheet

If you are writing science fiction or anything where you need to create a new world, then that world itself is sort of a character in your story. Here is a worksheet to help you get to know your world a little better.

Name of the world/city/land _____

How many people/creatures inhabit the world? _____

What are the physical descriptions of the inhabitants of the world? _____
_____

What is the age of the world? Is it a relatively new or ancient world? _____
_____

What language(s) do they speak? _____
_____

What are some of the dominant features of the culture? What do they value? What do they dismiss as not valuable? _____
_____

What does the landscape look like? _____
_____

How do the inhabitants divide themselves (city dwellers, country dwellers, upper class, lower class, mountain people, etc.)? _____
_____

Is there a form of racism in this society? If so, what does it look like? _____
_____
_____

How technologically advanced is the civilization? _____

What do the inhabitants do for entertainment? _____

What is the food like? _____

Is there any magical element to the world? _____

How does a typical family look/function? _____

What kind of weather does this world experience? _____

What is their point of view/belief system about God/religion/the universe? If they pray, who do they pray to and how? _____

How does this culture treat outsiders? _____

What are the healthy aspects of the society? _____

What are the unhealthy aspects of the society? _____

What has the history been? (Troubled, plagued by war, peaceful times, infighting, etc.) _____

Do they have any natural enemies and allies? _____

Any surprising rules? _____

Just Good to Know

Writers get point of view mixed up all the time. Here is a little quick and dirty explanation.

QUICK Point of View Go-To Guide

Types of Points of View: First Person, Third Person, Third Person Omniscient, Third Person Limited Omniscient and Multiple Points of View. People get them confused. Here's an easy breakdown:

First Person Point of View: First person uses the pronouns "I" or "we." First person is a limited point of view because it is limited to the person telling the story. The readers can never know more than what that one character knows or sees.

Third Person: Third person uses "she" or "he." The writer writes what he/she sees as an observer or what the character sees.

1. Third Person Omniscient: Can describe the actions, thoughts, feelings and intentions of all characters in all time periods. (Allows the writer to describe the thoughts and feelings of all characters.)

2. Third Person Limited: Sticks to the thoughts and feelings of one character and does not describe the thoughts of others (easiest to write and possibly the most commonly used).

3. Multiple Points of View: The writer tells the story from more than one point of view. This can be done in a variety of ways, sometimes switching points of view within chapters and other times switching points of view from one chapter to the next.

Here Are Some More...
Techniques to Deepen Characters

(I love this stuff, but my editor said the Character chapter was too long, so I'm sneaking it in here. It's all good stuff.)

- Dinner Guest Method
- Defense Mechanism
- The Monologue
- The Interview
- Childhood Memories from 5 to 15

DINNER GUEST Method

A quick tool to help define a character is to discover how your character would act at a dinner party. This is not a long, involved process. Simply think about how the host or hostess might describe your character (pick the word that most describes how your character would act).

He or she was

Quiet, loud, shy, chattering, flirty, giggly, drunk, pushy, depressed, angry, flamboyant, paranoid, fiery, scary, oppressive, hurtful, mean-spirited, intellectual, sweet, rude, hungry, humble, bossy, opinionated, giving, funny, smart, savvy, careful, awkward, nerdy, challenging, provocative, candid, sexual, snobby, violent, inquisitive, repressed, cold, clueless, manic, peppy, unpredictable, cautious, bold, out of place, self-centered, secretive...

THE DEFENSE MECHANISM (What Covers the Wound):

Your character's life-defining wound often creates a mask called a defense mechanism → this is what your character uses to hide behind.

According to Freud, a defense mechanism is an unconscious psychological strategy that the person uses to cope with their personal reality. Some defense mechanisms are healthy and some are not. Jung calls the mask a persona.

To put it simply: Your character will use their defense mechanisms to cope with their world. And often they do not know they are doing it!

Top 15 Examples of Defense Mechanisms

1. Using Humor (Hides behind joking/jokes, goofy personality.)
2. Repression ("I don't really want that," desire stuffed so far down the person is unaware, desire is in the unconscious.)
3. Denial (It's not real, doesn't exist, "I don't know what you're talking about!")
4. Creating Fantasies (Lives in world of her own making.)
5. Misdirecting Anger (Takes anger out on others or on wrong target.)
6. Shutting Down (Won't deal.)
7. Displacement (Attention on others or another topic.)
8. Blaming Others ("It's all his fault.")
9. Intellectualizing (Focusing on intellectual aspects to avoid dealing with emotion.)
10. Technologizing (My invention: Hiding behind computers, texting, phones, any technology as a coping mechanism.)
11. Isolating (Withdrawing from life and others.)

12. Idealization (Seeing a situation or person in its ideal form or as perfect to avoid dealing with a troubling reality.)
13. Passive Aggression (Anger toward others but not expressed directly, can be doing or saying something or avoiding doing or saying something such as procrastination, arriving late, forgetting.)
14. Hypochondriasis (Being preoccupied with being sick or worrying that one will be sick/ill.)
15. Rationalization (False reasoning: "Everything is fine." Often comes in the form of making excuses.)

Tips for Using the Defense Mechanism:

Use the character's defense mechanism until the character is ready to let down his guard and become/face his real self.

The defense mechanism is your character's "go-to mode" when under pressure.

Great dialogue can come from two characters speaking from their defense mechanisms. Think of two blamers having a talk. Or a blamer vs. a fantasy creator, a misdirecting anger vs. using humor, idealizing vs. blame, or hypochondriasis vs. fantasy thinking.

Write a MONOLOGUE:

Pick a topic like romance, heartbreak, career satisfaction, being a parent, addictions, most memorable life moments, etc., and have your character talk to an audience from his/her heart.

Monologue Prompts

The worst day of my career went like this:

I have never told anyone about the first time I got my heart broken. This is what happened:

I'm addicted to:

My childhood ended when:

The day I realized life doesn't happen the way you think it will was:

INTERVIEW Your Character:

This is a classic technique to deepen your character. Grab a pen and paper or your laptop. Select a few questions from the list below. You may be happily surprised by what you learn from the interview. You can also use automatic writing where you read a question: Without thinking or self-editing, just put pen to paper and write.

1. What do you regret most?
2. Do you have a moment you wish you could do over?
3. What person has made the biggest impact on your life?
4. Did you ever have a nickname?
5. Describe your physical looks. Would people agree with your assessment? Anything you'd want to change about your body?
6. Anyone you are dying to meet?
7. What does your dream house look like?
8. What stops you from living the life you really want to live?
9. What makes you quirky?
10. What skill do you wish you had?
11. What is your best and worst memory of your father growing up?

12. What is your best and worst memory of your mother growing up?
13. When you were six, what did you fear most?
14. Would you say that spiritually you believe what your parents believed? Why or why not?
15. What motivates you more than anything else?
16. Are you an introvert or an extrovert? Ever wish you were the opposite?
17. Ever been to a therapist? If so, for what issue? Did you learn anything about yourself?
18. What are your opinions on marriage, divorce, living together, children?
19. Who is your closest friend? How long have you been friends? What does this person give you?
20. Ever traveled? Favorite spot and worst spot.
21. Ultimate place to live in the world.
22. What occupation did you want to be when you were 10 and why? What led you to the occupation you are in now or heading toward?
23. How do you feel about money? What was the money situation when you were growing up?
24. Worst high school teacher, best high school experience.
25. Talent you wish you had.
26. If you could go back in time and visit yourself for a few minutes to deliver a message, what moment would you pick and what would you say?
27. Favorite movie and why? Favorite book, band, artist.
28. Who is the person you are most jealous of and why?
29. Who influenced your life the most in each decade? Who were your mentors?
30. If you could sing (professionally) what song would you choose and where would you sing it?

Childhood MEMORIES from 5 to 15

Write up a childhood memory for your character for every year from ages 5 to 15. What moments stand out in your character's life? Why?

They need not be long, just moments.

Example

5 - Dad deployed; we all helped him pack.
6 - Got to go to Disneyland; brothers picked all the rides.
7 - Got my first keyboard.
8 - Mom slapped me; older brother watched.
9 - Older brother went to college. Left while I was at school, forgot to say goodbye or leave me his keyboard.
10 - Dad came back from active duty—Mom and Dad fighting.
11 - Dad thought he got a job but he didn't; came home drunk.
12 - Brother got caught with drugs in school; I hid in my room when he and Dad fought.
13 - Got second keyboard; wrote first song. Dad told me I was wasting my time.
14 - Found Dad drunk in the middle of the day at the bar. Got into karate to defend myself against Dad.
15 - Started my own band. Met Sarah. Second brother left for army.

Books I Used to Create My Methods of Madness and That I Suggest You Read Too:

- *The Comic Toolbox* by John Vorhaus
- *The Hero's Journey* by Joseph Campbell
- *A Writer's Book of Days* by Judy Reeves
- *The Art of Dramatic Writing* by Lajos Egri
- *The Art and Craft of Playwriting* by Jeffrey Hatcher
- *The Writer's Journey* by Christopher Vogler
- *20 Master Plots* by Ronald B. Tobias
- *Writer's Guide to Character Traits* by Linda Edelstein
- *Save the Cat* by Blake Snyder
- *The Anatomy of Story* by John Truby
- *The War of Art: Break Through the Blocks and Win Your Inner Creative Battles* by Steven Pressfield
- *Man and his Symbols* or *The Archetypes and the Collective Unconscious* by Carl Jung

Acknowledgments and Credits

It takes a village to get a writing coach to write a book. Thanks to my village: Little Jimmy Freedman, Ben, Carlos, Uncle Billy, Kim, Phil, Brian, Edythe, Jessica Roach, Angela, Annie, Cathy, Jennifer, Madonna, Antoinette, Dan and Benni, Jill, Judy, Prema, Miguel, Kristen, Stephanie, Alex, Keiran, Jamie, Matt, Elea, Nicole, Jennifer, Lynn, Will, Noel, Sharon, Pita, Carlos Sr., Justin, Ed, Jaime, Fitz, Lex, Janey, Susan, Tracy, Alexa, Evan, Jordan, Vin, Aliah, Paz, Zack, Zsuzsi, Kristen, Lawrence, Maggie, Sophie, Melanie, Michelle, Nancy, Mandi, Rebecca, Tami, Robert, Sue, Etai, Heather, Marijke, Helen, Tanya, Vanessa, Sara, Victor, Kate, Scott, Roxzana, Rick, Danny, Jake, Shiloh, Ed, Ben, Jocelyn, Toni, Susan, Lex, Mike, Anastasia, Cherie, Daisy, Danielle, Delia, Donna, Karen, and Barb.

Special thanks to everyone at San Diego Writers, Ink and UCSD.

DEEP THANKS TO MY EDITORS!

Editors: Tracy Jones, Carlos de los Rios, Noel Dwyer, Andrea Glass

Book Cover Designer: Gwyn Kennedy Snider at GKS Creative www.gkscreative.com

Special Note: Some of the writers' names have been changed to protect the innocent.

Photo/Illustration Credits

INFOGRAPHICS: Alfredo Guida
Copyright: <a href='http://www.123rf.com/profile_xochicalco'>xochicalco / 123RF Stock Photo</a>
Copyright: <a href='http://www.123rf.com/profile_tribalium123'>tribalium123 / 123RF Stock Photo</a>

Copyright: <a href='http://www.123rf.com/profile_yupiramos'>yupiramos / 123RF Stock Photo</a>
Copyright: <a href='http://www.123rf.com/profile_lineartestpilot'>lineartestpilot / 123RF Stock Photo</a>
Copyright: <a href='http://www.123rf.com/profile_indomercy'>indomercy / 123RF Stock Photo</a>
Copyright: <a href='http://www.123rf.com/profile_dvarg'>dvarg / 123RF Stock Photo</a>
Copyright: <a href='http://www.123rf.com/profile_graphicsdunia4you'>graphicsdunia4you / 123RF Stock Photo</a>
Copyright: <a href='http://www.123rf.com/profile_vadimmmus'>vadimmmus / 123RF Stock Photo</a>
Copyright: <a href='http://www.123rf.com/profile_file404'>file404 / 123RF Stock Photo</a>
Copyright: <a href='http://www.123rf.com/profile_boohoo'>boohoo / 123RF Stock Photo</a>
Copyright: <a href='http://www.123rf.com/profile_volhabelausava'>volhabelausava / 123RF Stock Photo</a>
Copyright: <a href='http://www.123rf.com/profile_vivat191192'>vivat191192 / 123RF Stock Photo</a>
Copyright: <a href='http://www.123rf.com/profile_morphart'>morphart / 123RF Stock Photo</a>
Copyright: <a href='http://www.123rf.com/profile_lineartestpilot'>lineartestpilot / 123RF Stock Photo</a>
Copyright: <a href='http://www.123rf.com/profile_siamimages'>siamimages / 123RF Stock Photo</a>
Copyright: <a href='http://www.123rf.com/profile_izakowski'>izakowski / 123RF Stock Photo</a>
Copyright: <a href='http://www.123rf.com/profile_pixelbird'>pixelbird / 123RF Stock Photo</a>
Copyright: <a href='http://www.123rf.com/profile_quka'>quka / 123RF Stock Photo</a>
Copyright: <a href='http://www.123rf.com/profile_hchjjl'>hchjjl / 123RF Stock Photo</a>
Copyright: <a href='http://www.123rf.com/profile_donatas1205'>donatas1205 / 123RF Stock Photo</a>
Copyright: <a href='http://www.123rf.com/profile_liubomirt'>liubomirt / 123RF Stock Photo</a>
Copyright: <a href='http://www.123rf.com/profile_meisenhut'>meisenhut / 123RF Stock Photo</a>
Copyright: <a href='http://www.123rf.com/profile_apostrophe'>apostrophe / 123RF Stock Photo</a>
Copyright: <a href='http://www.123rf.com/profile_aaronamat'>aaronamat / 123RF Stock Photo</a>
Copyright: <a href='http://www.123rf.com/profile_vlue'>vlue / 123RF Stock Photo</a>

Copyright: <a href='http://www.123rf.com/profile_aroas'>aroas / 123RF Stock Photo</a>
Copyright: <a href='http://www.123rf.com/profile_tommasolizzul'>tommasolizzul / 123RF Stock Photo</a>
Copyright: <a href='http://www.123rf.com/profile_blueringmedia'>blueringmedia / 123RF Stock Photo</a>
Copyright: <a href='http://www.123rf.com/profile_leolintang'>leolintang / 123RF Stock Photo</a>
Copyright: <a href='http://www.123rf.com/profile_albertzig'>albertzig / 123RF Stock Photo</a>
Copyright: <a href='http://www.123rf.com/profile_1enchik'>1enchik / 123RF Stock Photo</a>
Copyright: <a href='http://www.123rf.com/profile_chuhail'>chuhail / 123RF Stock Photo</a>
Copyright: <a href='http://www.123rf.com/profile_johan2011'>johan2011 / 123RF Stock Photo</a>
Copyright: <a href='http://www.123rf.com/profile_aaabbbccc'>aaabbbccc / 123RF Stock Photo</a>
Copyright: <a href='http://www.123rf.com/profile_retroclipart'>retroclipart / 123RF Stock Photo</a>
Copyright: <a href='http://www.123rf.com/profile_perysty'>perysty / 123RF Stock Photo</a>
Copyright: <a href='http://www.123rf.com/profile_emattil'>emattil / 123RF Stock Photo</a>
Copyright: <a href='http://www.123rf.com/profile_Krisdog'>Krisdog / 123RF Stock Photo</a>
Copyright: <a href='http://www.123rf.com/profile_orson'>orson / 123RF Stock Photo</a>
Copyright: <a href='http://www.123rf.com/profile_aleksander1'>aleksander1 / 123RF Stock Photo</a
Copyright: <a href='http://www.123rf.com/profile_deepfuze'>deepfuze / 123RF Stock Photo</a>
Copyright: <a href='http://www.123rf.com/profile_pozitiw'>pozitiw / 123RF Stock Photo</a>
Copyright: <a href='http://www.123rf.com/profile_loopall'>loopall / 123RF Stock Photo</a>
Copyright: <a href='http://www.123rf.com/profile_vectorchef'>vectorchef / 123RF Stock Photo</a>
Copyright: <a href='http://www.123rf.com/profile_pupkis'>pupkis / 123RF Stock Photo</a>
Copyright: <a href='http://www.123rf.com/profile_jiripravda'>jiripravda / 123RF Stock Photo</a>
Copyright: <a href='http://www.123rf.com/profile_nitzman'>nitzman / 123RF Stock Photo</a
Copyright: <a href='http://www.123rf.com/profile_mtkang'>mtkang / 123RF Stock Photo</a>